W9-CAG-107

BETTER HOMES AND GARDENS®

COOKING FOR TODAY
MUFFINS & BREADS

BETTER HOMES AND GARDENS® BOOKS
Des Moines

BETTER HOMES AND GARDENS® BOOKS
An Imprint of Meredith® Books

MUFFINS & BREADS
Editors: Lisa Mannes, Mary Major Williams
Writer: Patricia A. Ward
Associate Art Director: Tom Wegner
Electronic Production Coordinator: Paula Forest
Test Kitchen Product Supervisors: Diana Nolin, Colleen Weeden
Food Stylists: Lynn Blanchard, Janet Pittman, Jennifer Peterson
Photographers: Mike Dieter, Scott Little
Production Manager: Douglas Johnston

Vice President and Editorial Director: Elizabeth P. Rice
Executive Editor: Kay Sanders
Art Director: Ernest Shelton
Managing Editor: Christopher Cavanaugh
Test Kitchen Director: Sharon Stilwell

President, Book Group: Joseph J. Ward
Vice President, Retail Marketing: Jamie L. Martin
Vice President, Direct Marketing: Timothy Jarrell

On the cover: Raspberry Almond Coffee Cake (see recipe, page 103)

Meredith Corporation
Chairman of the Executive Committee: E. T. Meredith III
Chairman of the Board and Chief Executive Officer: Jack D. Rehm
President and Chief Operating Officer: William T. Kerr

WE CARE!

All of us at Better Homes and Gardens® Books are dedicated to providing you with the information and ideas you need to create delicious foods. We welcome your comments and suggestions. Write to us at: Better Homes and Gardens® Books, Cookbook Editorial Department, RW-240, 1716 Locust St., Des Moines, IA 50309-3023

If you would like to order additional copies of any of our books, call 1-800-678-2803 or check with your local bookstore.

Our seal assures you that every recipe in *Cooking For Today: Muffins & Breads* has been tested in the Better Homes and Gardens® Test Kitchen. This means that each recipe is practical and reliable, and meets our high standards of taste appeal. We guarantee your satisfaction with this book for as long as you own it.

© Copyright 1995 by Meredith Corporation, Des Moines, Iowa.
All rights reserved. Printed in the United States of America.
First Edition. Printing Number and Year: 5 4 3 2 1 99 98 97 96 95
Library of Congress Catalog Card Number: 95-75617
ISBN: 0-696-20097-X

Freshly baked bread, whether made with yeast or some other leavening, is hard to resist. Even before you taste the bread, you're rewarded with its aroma.

More than half of the recipes in this cookbook are quick breads. Each can be mixed up and baked in no time. Don't miss the twenty muffin recipes, all moist and bursting with flavor. Prepare the tea breads, too, but remember they're best made in advance and stored overnight before slicing.

Afternoon tea or morning coffee wouldn't be complete without light, flaky biscuits or scones, and you have a baker's dozen to choose from. We've divided the coffee cakes into yeast and quick breads, giving you the option to choose the type that best fits your day.

In this collection, you'll find all kinds of yeast breads, from a sturdy country rye loaf that starts with an old-fashioned rye sponge to cinnamon rolls glistening with vanilla icing that rise to perfection after a night in the refrigerator.

We hope you'll find these 68 kitchen-tested recipes a source of pleasure for your guests or family and a source of pride for you.

CONTENTS

QUICK BREADS

MUFFIN & QUICK-BREAD TIPS

■ To keep the edges of your muffins and quick breads nicely rounded, grease the muffin cups or baking pans on the bottoms and only ½ inch up sides.

■ After adding the liquid mixture to the flour mixture, stir just till moistened. If you stir till the batter is smooth, your muffins and quick breads will have a tough texture.

■ Be sure to bake muffin and quick-bread batter right away. Batters with baking powder and/or baking soda lose leavening power if not baked immediately.

■ To avoid soggy sides and bottoms, cool muffins and quick breads in baking pans only as long as directed in the recipe.

BISCUIT & SCONE TIPS

■ Avoid over mixing the fat with the flour. Over mixing produces mealy biscuits and scones rather than flaky ones. Always use chilled margarine or butter because it's easier to cut into the flour and get coarse crumbs.

■ Do not over knead the dough. Folding and pressing the dough gently for 10 to 12 strokes is enough to distribute moisture.

■ Cut as many biscuits and scones as possible from a single rolling of the dough. The extra flour needed for rerolling will cause biscuits and scones to be dry.

■ Biscuits and scones are done when both the bottom and top crusts are an even golden brown.

YEAST BREADS

YEAST-BREAD TIPS

■ Baking with yeast can be tricky even for experienced bakers. Yeast dough that is too hot or too cold won't rise properly. For best results, use a thermometer to check the temperature of the liquids before mixing and choose a warm, but not hot, area for raising dough.

■ Kneading dough can be messy when you use too little flour or difficult if you use too much. We give a range for the amount of flour to use. Just start with the minimum amount and add a little at a time till the dough is easily kneaded.

■ Let the dough rise in a draft-free area with a temperature range of 80° to 85°. Your oven is a great place for raising dough. Place the bowl of dough in an unheated oven and set a large pan of hot water under the bowl on the oven's lower rack.

■ An easy way to check the bread for doneness is by tapping the top of the loaf with your finger. If it sounds hollow, the bread is done. Rolls and coffee cakes are done when their tops are golden brown.

DOUGH STIFFNESS

■ The right stiffness of the dough is important. Knead the dough the suggested amount of time and identify the right dough stiffness for the recipe.
■ Moderately soft dough is slightly sticky and may be kneaded on a floured surface. It's used for most sweet breads and coffee cakes.
■ Moderately stiff dough is not sticky but yields slightly to the touch. It kneads easily on a floured surface and is used for most unsweet breads.
■ Stiff dough is firm to the touch and kneads easily on a lightly floured surface. This type of dough is used for a chewy-textured bread.

YEAST-BREAD TECHNIQUES

Kneading: Place dough on a lightly floured surface. Knead by folding the dough and pushing it down with the heels of your hands, curving your fingers over the dough. Turn, fold, and push down again.

Rising: Check if the dough has doubled and is ready for shaping by pressing two fingers ½ inch into the dough. Remove your fingers. If the indentations remain, the dough has doubled and it is ready to be punched down.

Punching down the dough: Push your fist into the center of the dough, pressing beyond the surface. Pull the edges of the dough to the center. Turn the dough over and place it on a lightly floured surface.

MORE ABOUT YEAST

■ You can substitute quick-rising yeast for active dry yeast in equal measures in practically every yeast recipe in this book. Exceptions are recipes made with sourdough starter, a sponge, or those recipes requiring refrigeration before baking. Quick-rise yeast dough should rise in about a third less time. Check the manufacturer's directions for the water temperature to use because it might differ from the recipe using active dry yeast.
■ Store packets of dry yeast in a cool, dry place and the yeast will stay fresh till the expiration date stamped on the package. If you buy jars of loose yeast, store in a cool, dry place till opened, then refrigerate tightly covered.

GIANT BLUEBERRY MUFFINS

If you prefer a dozen smaller muffins, spoon batter into twelve 2½-inch muffin pan cups and bake in a 375° oven for 20 minutes or till golden.

2 cups all-purpose flour
¾ cup sugar
2½ teaspoons baking powder
½ teaspoon salt
2 beaten eggs
¾ cup milk
½ cup melted butter or margarine or cooking oil
1 tablespoon finely shredded orange peel
1 cup fresh or frozen blueberries, thawed
Coarse sugar (optional)

Grease six 1-cup muffin cups. Set muffin cups aside.

In a medium mixing bowl stir together flour, sugar, baking powder, and salt. Make a well in the center of dry mixture.

In another medium mixing bowl combine eggs; milk; margarine, butter, or oil; and orange peel. Add all at once to the dry mixture. Stir just till moistened (batter should be lumpy). Fold in blueberries.

Spoon batter into the prepared muffin cups, filling each almost full. If desired, sprinkle tops with coarse sugar. Bake in a 350° oven about 35 minutes or till golden. Cool in muffin cups on a wire rack for 5 minutes. Then remove muffins from muffin cups. Serve warm. Makes 6 large muffins.

Nutrition facts per muffin: 425 calories, 18 g total fat (10 g saturated fat), 114 mg cholesterol, 522 mg sodium, 60 g carbohydrate, 2 g fiber, 7 g protein.
Daily value: 19% vitamin A, 8% vitamin C, 16% calcium, 15% iron.

BANANA ALMOND MUFFINS

Put those ripe bananas to good use in this flavorful muffin recipe. You can freeze mashed bananas in 1-cup amounts till you're ready to mix up a batch. Just thaw and use.

1½ cups all-purpose flour
½ cup sugar
3 tablespoons toasted wheat germ
1½ teaspoons baking powder
½ teaspoon salt
¼ teaspoon baking soda
2 beaten eggs
½ cup cooking oil
3 ripe medium bananas, mashed (1 cup)
½ cup toasted chopped almonds
1 tablespoon sugar
¼ teaspoon ground cinnamon

Grease twelve 2½-inch muffin cups or line with paper bake cups. Set muffin cups aside.

In a medium mixing bowl stir together flour, ½ cup sugar, wheat germ, baking powder, salt, and baking soda. Make a well in the center of dry mixture.

In another medium mixing bowl combine the eggs, oil, and bananas. Add all at once to the dry mixture. Stir just till moistened (batter should be lumpy). Fold in almonds.

Spoon batter into the prepared muffin cups, filling each ⅔ full. For topping, combine 1 tablespoon sugar and cinnamon. Sprinkle over batter. Bake in a 400° oven about 20 minutes or till golden. Cool in muffin cups on a wire rack for 5 minutes. Then remove muffins from muffin cups. Serve warm. Makes 12.

Nutrition facts per muffin: 240 calories, 13 g total fat (2 g saturated fat), 36 mg cholesterol, 172 mg sodium, 29 g carbohydrate, 1 g fiber, 5 g protein.
Daily value: 1% vitamin A, 4% vitamin C, 5% calcium, 8% iron.

PEAR, GINGER, AND WALNUT MUFFINS

Chunks of pears and walnuts make these muffins real winners. The unusual addition of grated gingerroot makes them extra special.

2   cups all-purpose flour
¾   cup sugar
2   teaspoons baking powder
½   teaspoon salt
¼   teaspoon ground cardamom or
        1 teaspoon ground cinnamon
2   beaten eggs
½   cup cooking oil
2   tablespoons milk
1   teaspoon grated gingerroot
2   medium pears, peeled, cored, and
        finely chopped (1½ cups)
¾   cup chopped walnuts
½   cup raisins

Grease eighteen 2½-inch muffin cups or line with paper bake cups. Set muffin cups aside.

In a medium mixing bowl stir together flour, sugar, baking powder, salt, and cardamom or cinnamon. Make a well in the center of dry mixture.

In another medium mixing bowl combine eggs, oil, milk, and gingerroot. Add all at once to the dry mixture. Stir just till moistened (batter should be lumpy). Fold in pears, walnuts, and raisins.

Spoon batter into the prepared muffin cups, filling each ⅔ full. Bake in a 350° oven for 20 to 25 minutes or till golden. Cool in muffin cups on a wire rack for 5 minutes. Then remove muffins from muffin cups. Serve warm. Makes 18.

Nutrition facts per muffin: 197 calories, 10 g total fat (1 g saturated fat), 24 mg cholesterol, 118 mg sodium, 25 g carbohydrate, 1 g fiber, 3 g protein.
Daily value: 1% vitamin A, 1% vitamin C, 4% calcium, 6% iron.

CORNMEAL BRAN MUFFINS

Choose this recipe when you need extra muffins. This recipe turns out 18 average-sized ones.

1¼ cups whole bran cereal
1½ cups milk
½ cup whole wheat flour
½ cup all-purpose flour
½ cup yellow cornmeal
2 teaspoons baking powder
¼ teaspoon baking soda
¼ teaspoon salt
1 beaten egg
½ cup cooking oil
⅓ cup packed brown sugar
¾ cup raisins or currants
½ cup chopped walnuts or pecans

In a medium mixing bowl stir together cereal and milk and let stand 5 minutes. Meanwhile, grease eighteen 2½-inch muffin cups or corn stick pans. (Or, line muffin cups with paper bake cups.) Set aside.

In a medium mixing bowl stir together whole wheat flour, all-purpose flour, cornmeal, baking powder, baking soda, and salt. Make a well in the center of dry mixture.

In another medium mixing bowl combine egg, oil, and brown sugar. Stir in bran mixture. Add all at once to the dry mixture. Stir just till moistened (batter should be lumpy). Fold in raisins or currants and walnuts or pecans.

Spoon batter into the prepared muffin cups, filling each ⅔ full. Bake in a 400° oven about 20 minutes or till golden. Cool in muffin cups on a wire rack for 5 minutes. Then remove muffins from pans. Serve warm. Makes 18.

Nutrition facts per muffin: 162 calories, 9 g total fat (1 g saturated fat), 13 mg cholesterol, 135 mg sodium, 21 g carbohydrate, 2 g fiber, 3 g protein.
Daily value: 1% vitamin A, 8% vitamin C, 6% calcium, 9% iron.

CRANBERRY APPLE MUFFINS

Here's a great way to use leftover holiday cranberry sauce. But, don't wait for the holidays to make these, they're good all year round.

½ cup whole cranberry sauce
½ teaspoon finely shredded orange peel
1½ cups all-purpose flour
½ cup sugar
1 teaspoon ground cinnamon
½ teaspoon baking soda
¼ teaspoon baking powder
¼ teaspoon salt
1 beaten egg
⅓ cup milk
⅓ cup cooking oil
1 cup shredded peeled apple

Grease twelve 2½-inch muffin cups or line with paper bake cups. Set muffin cups aside.

In a small mixing bowl stir together cranberry sauce and orange peel. Set aside.

In a medium mixing bowl stir together flour, sugar, cinnamon, baking soda, baking powder, and salt. Make a well in the center of dry mixture.

In another medium mixing bowl combine egg, milk, and oil. Add all at once to the dry mixture. Stir just till moistened (batter should be lumpy). Fold in apple.

Spoon batter into the prepared muffin cups, filling each ⅔ full. Make an indentation in the center of each with the back of a spoon. Spoon *2 teaspoons* of cranberry mixture into each indentation. Bake in a 375° oven for 18 to 20 minutes or till golden. Cool in muffin cups on a wire rack for 5 minutes. Then remove muffins from muffin cups. Serve warm. Makes 12.

Nutrition facts per muffin: 172 calories, 7 g total fat (1 g saturated fat), 18 mg cholesterol, 117 mg sodium, 26 g carbohydrate, 1 g fiber, 2 g protein.
Daily value: 1% vitamin A, 1% vitamin C, 1% calcium, 5% iron.

CARROT SPICE MUFFINS

If you are using a cast iron pan, such as the one shown in the photograph, grease the pan and then preheat it in the oven for 5 minutes just before filling.

1¾ cups all-purpose flour
1½ teaspoons baking powder
1½ teaspoons pumpkin pie spice
¼ teaspoon baking soda
¼ teaspoon salt
1 beaten egg
¾ cup buttermilk
½ cup packed brown sugar
¼ cup cooking oil
1½ cups finely shredded carrots
¼ cup chopped walnuts or pecans
4 teaspoons granulated sugar

Grease twelve 2½-inch muffin cups or line with paper bake cups. Set muffin cups aside.

In a medium mixing bowl stir together flour, baking powder, pumpkin pie spice, baking soda, and salt. Make a well in the center of dry mixture.

In another medium mixing bowl combine the egg, buttermilk, brown sugar, and oil. Add egg mixture and carrots all at once to the dry mixture. Stir just till moistened (batter should be lumpy).

Spoon batter into the prepared muffin cups, filling each ⅔ full. In a small mixing bowl combine walnuts or pecans and granulated sugar. Sprinkle over batter. Bake in a 400° oven for 15 to 20 minutes or till golden. Cool in muffin cups on a wire rack for 5 minutes. Then remove muffins from muffin cups. Serve warm. Makes 12.

Nutrition facts per muffin: 170 calories, 7 g total fat (1 g saturated fat), 18 mg cholesterol, 145 mg sodium, 24 g carbohydrate, 1 g fiber, 3 g protein.
Daily value: 39% vitamin A, 2% vitamin C, 6% calcium, 8% iron.

BACON WALNUT MUFFINS

Bacon and thyme give a pleasant flavor blend to these savory muffins—great with salads or soups.

2¼ cups all-purpose flour
  2 teaspoons baking powder
  1 teaspoon snipped fresh thyme or
      ¼ teaspoon dried thyme leaves,
      crushed
  ⅛ teaspoon salt
  2 beaten eggs
  1 cup milk
  ½ cup cooking oil
  6 strips bacon, cooked, drained, and
      crumbled
  ½ cup chopped walnuts

Grease twelve 2½-inch muffin cups. Set muffin cups aside.

In a medium mixing bowl stir together flour, baking powder, thyme, and salt. Make a well in the center of dry mixture.

In another medium mixing bowl combine eggs, milk, and oil. Add all at once to the dry mixture. Stir just till moistened (batter should be lumpy). Fold in crumbled bacon and walnuts.

Spoon batter into the prepared muffin cups, filling each almost full. Bake in a 400° oven about 20 minutes or till golden. Cool in muffin cups on a wire rack for 5 minutes. Remove muffins from muffin cups. Serve warm. Makes 12.

Nutrition facts per muffin: 232 calories, 15 g total fat (3 g saturated fat), 40 mg cholesterol, 155 mg sodium, 19 g carbohydrate, 1 g fiber, 6 g protein.
Daily value: 2% vitamin A, 2% vitamin C, 7% calcium, 9% iron.

APPLE BUTTER MUFFINS

These gently spiced, moist muffins are best served warm with a smear of sweet butter.

1¾   cups all-purpose flour
½   cup packed brown sugar
2   teaspoons baking powder
1   teaspoon ground cinnamon
½   teaspoon salt
½   cup shortening
1   beaten egg
¾   cup milk
½   cup chopped pecans or walnuts
½   cup apple butter
1   tablespoon granulated sugar
¼   teaspoon ground cinnamon

Grease twelve 2½-inch muffin cups or line with paper bake cups. Set muffin cups aside.

In a medium mixing bowl stir together flour, brown sugar, baking powder, 1 teaspoon cinnamon, and salt. Cut in shortening till mixture resembles coarse crumbs.

In a small mixing bowl combine egg and milk. Add all at once to the dry mixture. Stir just till moistened (batter should be lumpy). Fold in pecans or walnuts.

Spoon *2 tablespoons* of the batter into each prepared muffin cup. Top each with *2 teaspoons* of the apple butter. Spoon about *2 tablespoons* more of the batter on top of the apple butter.

For topping, combine granulated sugar and ¼ teaspoon cinnamon. Sprinkle topping over batter. Bake in a 400° oven about 20 minutes or till golden. Cool in muffin cups on a wire rack for 5 minutes. Then remove muffins from muffin cups. Serve warm. Makes 12.

Nutrition facts per muffin: 238 calories, 13 g total fat (3 g saturated fat), 19 mg cholesterol, 165 mg sodium, 29 g carbohydrate, 1 g fiber, 3 g protein.
Daily value: 1% vitamin A, 0% vitamin C, 7% calcium, 9% iron.

PEACH-FILLED WHEAT MUFFINS

Enjoy these whole wheat-flavored muffins with a surprise center of preserves. Each time you make these, you can use different types of preserves, such as raspberry, strawberry, or cherry.

1 cup all-purpose flour
½ cup whole wheat flour
½ cup sugar
1¼ teaspoons baking powder
¼ teaspoon baking soda
¼ teaspoon salt
1 beaten egg
1 8-ounce carton dairy sour cream
¼ cup cooking oil
½ cup toasted chopped pecans (optional)
¼ cup peach preserves

Line twelve 2½-inch muffin cups with paper bake cups. Set muffin cups aside.

In a medium mixing bowl stir together all-purpose flour, whole wheat flour, sugar, baking powder, baking soda, and salt. Make a well in the center of dry mixture.

In another medium mixing bowl combine the egg, sour cream, and oil. Add all at once to the dry mixture. Stir just till moistened. Fold in pecans, if desired.

Spoon about *half* of the batter into the prepared muffin cups, filling each ⅓ full. Top *each* with *1 teaspoon* of the peach preserves. Then top with remaining batter, filling ⅔ full. Bake in a 400° oven for 18 to 20 minutes or till golden. Cool in muffin cups on a wire rack for 5 minutes. Then remove muffins from muffin cups. Serve warm. Makes 12.

Nutrition facts per muffin: 189 calories, 9 g total fat (3 g saturated fat), 26 mg cholesterol, 125 mg sodium, 25 g carbohydrate, 1 g fiber, 3 g protein.
Daily value: 5% vitamin A, 0% vitamin C, 5% calcium, 5% iron.

LEMON-GLAZED PISTACHIO MUFFINS

Before you glaze these flavorful muffins, place them on a wire rack over waxed paper or foil. Cleanup will be a snap.

1   cup all-purpose flour
½   cup whole wheat flour
½   cup sugar
2   teaspoons baking powder
¼   teaspoon salt
1   beaten egg
½   cup milk
¼   cup cooking oil
1   teaspoon finely shredded lemon peel
¾   cup chopped pistachios
    Lemon Glaze

Grease twelve 2½-inch muffin cups or line with paper bake cups. Set muffin cups aside.

In a medium mixing bowl stir together all-purpose flour, whole wheat flour, sugar, baking powder, and salt. Make a well in the center of dry mixture.

In another medium mixing bowl combine egg, milk, oil, and lemon peel. Add all at once to the dry mixture. Stir just till moistened (batter should be lumpy). Fold in pistachios.

Spoon batter into the prepared muffin cups, filling each ⅔ full. Bake in a 375° oven for 18 to 20 minutes or till golden. Cool in muffin cups on a wire rack for 5 minutes. Remove muffins from muffin cups. Brush or drizzle with Lemon Glaze. Serve warm. Makes 12.

Lemon Glaze: In a small mixing bowl stir together ½ cup sifted *powdered sugar* and ½ teaspoon *lemon juice*. Mix till smooth. If necessary, stir in a little water to make drizzling consistency.

Nutrition facts per muffin: 198 calories, 9 g total fat (1 g saturated fat), 19 mg cholesterol, 116 mg sodium, 26 g carbohydrate, 2 g fiber, 4 g protein.
Daily value: 1% vitamin A, 1% vitamin C, 7% calcium, 8% iron.

WHOLE KERNEL CORN MUFFINS

These cornmeal muffins have a Southwestern flair. The cornmeal gives them a slightly sweet flavor and a crumbly texture.

1   cup all-purpose flour
¾   cup cornmeal
3   tablespoons sugar
2   teaspoons baking powder
¼   teaspoon salt
1   beaten egg
¾   cup milk
¼   cup cooking oil
1   8¾-ounce can whole kernel corn,
       drained
2   tablespoons snipped fresh chives or
       finely chopped green onion

Grease twelve 2½-inch muffin cups. Set muffin cups aside.

In a medium mixing bowl stir together flour, cornmeal, sugar, baking powder, and salt. Make a well in the center of dry mixture.

In another medium mixing bowl combine egg, milk, and oil. Add all at once to the dry mixture. Stir just till moistened (batter should be lumpy). Fold in corn and chives or green onion.

Spoon batter into the prepared muffin cups, filling each ⅔ full. Bake in a 400° oven for 18 to 20 minutes or till golden. Cool in muffin cups on wire racks for 5 minutes. Then remove muffins from muffin cups. Serve warm. Makes 12.

Nutrition facts per muffin: 144 calories, 6 g total fat (1 g saturated fat), 19 mg cholesterol, 163 mg sodium, 21 g carbohydrate, 1 g fiber, 3 g protein.
Daily value: 2% vitamin A, 2% vitamin C, 6% calcium, 7% iron.

FRUITED SPICY MUFFINS

If you prefer, use a mix of snipped dried fruit; measure out ⅔ cup of your favorite combination.

1½ cups all-purpose flour
¾ cup quick-cooking oats
½ cup sugar
2 teaspoons baking powder
2 teaspoons pumpkin pie spice
¼ teaspoon salt
1 beaten egg
¾ cup milk
¼ cup cooking oil
⅓ cup snipped dried apricots, cherries, or peaches
⅓ cup snipped pitted prunes or dates
⅓ cup chopped walnuts

Grease twelve 2½-inch muffin cups or line with paper bake cups. Set muffin cups aside.

In a medium mixing bowl stir together flour, quick-cooking oats, sugar, baking powder, pumpkin pie spice, and salt. Make a well in the center of the dry mixture.

In another medium mixing bowl combine egg, milk, and oil. Add all at once to the dry mixture. Stir just till moistened (batter should be lumpy). Fold in apricots, cherries, or peaches; prunes or dates; and chopped walnuts.

Spoon batter into the prepared muffin cups, filling each ⅔ full. Bake in a 400° oven for 20 to 25 minutes or till golden. Cool in muffin cups on a wire rack for 5 minutes. Then remove muffins from muffin cups. Serve warm. Makes 12.

Nutrition facts per muffin: 200 calories, 8 g total fat (1 g saturated fat), 19 mg cholesterol, 119 mg sodium, 29 g carbohydrate, 2 g fiber, 4 g protein.
Daily value: 5% vitamin A, 0% vitamin C, 7% calcium, 9% iron.

SUGAR-TOPPED LEMON POPPY SEED MUFFINS

Bakers have been using poppy seed to decorate cakes and breads since the days of the ancient Egyptians and Romans. We've used them here to add both flavor and texture.

1¾ cups all-purpose flour
½ cup sugar
1 tablespoon poppy seed
1 tablespoon finely shredded lemon peel
2 teaspoons baking powder
½ teaspoon salt
1 beaten egg
¾ cup milk
¼ cup cooking oil
2 tablespoons butter or margarine, melted
2 tablespoons sugar

Grease twelve 2½-inch muffin cups or line with paper bake cups. Set muffin cups aside.

In a medium mixing bowl stir together flour, ½ cup sugar, poppy seed, lemon peel, baking powder, and salt. Make a well in the center of dry mixture.

In another medium bowl combine egg, milk, and oil. Add all at once to the dry mixture. Stir just till moistened (batter should be lumpy).

Spoon batter into the prepared muffin cups, filling each ⅔ full. Bake in a 375° oven for 20 to 25 minutes or till golden. Cool in muffin cups on a wire rack for 5 minutes. Remove muffins from muffin cups. Dip tops of muffins into melted butter or margarine, then into the 2 tablespoons sugar to lightly coat. Serve warm. Makes 12.

Nutrition facts per muffin: 177 calories, 8 g total fat (1 g saturated fat), 19 mg cholesterol, 185 mg sodium, 24 g carbohydrate, 0 g fiber, 3 g protein.
Daily value: 4% vitamin A, 1% vitamin C, 7% calcium, 6% iron.

ZUCCHINI RAISIN WHEAT MUFFINS

These extra-moist muffins are heartier than most because they start with whole wheat flour. The zucchini and raisins add lots of flavor.

1	cup all-purpose flour
1	cup whole wheat flour
2	teaspoons baking powder
1	teaspoon ground cinnamon
½	teaspoon salt
⅛	teaspoon ground cloves
½	cup butter or margarine
½	cup packed brown sugar
2	beaten eggs
¼	cup milk
1½	cups finely shredded zucchini
½	cup snipped light raisins or currants

Grease twelve 2½-inch muffin cups or line with paper bake cups. Set muffin cups aside.

In a medium mixing bowl stir together all-purpose flour, whole wheat flour, baking powder, cinnamon, salt, and cloves.

In a large mixing bowl beat butter or margarine with an electric mixer on medium speed about 30 seconds or till softened. Add the brown sugar, beating till light and fluffy. Add eggs, one at a time, beating till combined. Beat in milk. Add flour mixture and zucchini. Stir till combined. Stir in raisins or currants.

Spoon batter into the prepared muffin cups, filling each almost full. Bake in a 375° oven for 20 to 25 minutes or till golden. Cool in muffin cups on a wire rack for 5 minutes. Then remove muffins from muffin cups. Serve warm. Makes 12.

Nutrition facts per muffin: 202 calories, 9 g total fat (5 g saturated fat), 56 mg cholesterol, 244 mg sodium, 28 g carbohydrate, 2 g fiber, 4 g protein.
Daily value: *9% vitamin A, 2% vitamin C, 7% calcium, 9% iron.*

STREUSEL CHERRY MUFFIN TOPS

Muffin-top or muffin-crown pans make flat muffin rounds. Look for these pans in specialty cookware stores or department stores.

1¾ cups all-purpose flour
2 teaspoons baking powder
¼ teaspoon salt
1 beaten egg
¾ cup milk
½ cup packed brown sugar
¼ cup butter or margarine, melted
1 cup pitted, chopped fresh sweet cherries or chopped frozen sweet cherries
¼ cup chopped almonds
   Streusel Topping

Grease 9 muffin-top cups. Set muffin cups aside.

In a medium mixing bowl stir together flour, baking powder, and salt. Make a well in the center of dry mixture.

In another medium bowl combine egg, milk, brown sugar, and butter or margarine. Add all at once to the dry mixture. Stir just till moistened (batter should be lumpy). Fold in cherries and almonds.

Spoon batter into the prepared muffin-top cups, filling each almost full. Sprinkle with Streusel Topping. Bake in 375° oven for 10 to 13 minutes or till golden. Cool in muffin cups on a wire rack for 5 minutes. Then remove muffins from muffin cups. Serve warm. Makes 9.

Streusel Topping: In small bowl combine ½ cup packed *brown sugar,* ¼ cup *quick-cooking oats,* 2 tablespoons *all-purpose flour,* and 2 tablespoons melted *butter* or *margarine.* Mix till crumbly.

Nutrition facts per muffin: 288 calories, 11 g total fat (5 g saturated fat), 46 mg cholesterol, 241 mg sodium, 45 g carbohydrate, 2 g fiber, 5 g protein.
Daily value: 9% vitamin A, 2% vitamin C, 11% calcium, 13% iron.

Streusel Cherry Muffins: Prepare as directed above except grease twelve 2½-inch muffin cups or line with paper bake cups. Spoon batter into prepared muffin cups, filling each ⅔ full. Bake in a 375° for 20 to 25 minutes or till golden. Cool as above. Makes 12.

Nutrition facts per muffin: 216 calories, 8 g total fat (4 g saturated fat), 34 mg cholesterol, 181 mg sodium, 33 g carbohydrate, 1 g fiber, 4 g protein.
Daily value: 7% vitamin A, 2% vitamin C, 8% calcium, 10% iron.

NUTMEG-GLAZED GINGERBREAD MUFFINS

These nicely spiced muffins are marvelous served warm with whipped honey butter. Combine some honey with softened butter and beat till blended.

1¾ cups all-purpose flour
2 teaspoons baking powder
1 teaspoon ground cinnamon
¾ teaspoon ground ginger
¼ teaspoon baking soda
1 beaten egg
⅔ cup milk
¼ cup packed brown sugar
¼ cup cooking oil
¼ cup light molasses
   Nutmeg Glaze

Grease twelve 2½-inch muffin cups or line with paper bake cups. Set muffin cups aside.

In a medium mixing bowl stir together flour, baking powder, cinnamon, ginger, and baking soda. Make a well in the center of dry mixture.

In another medium mixing bowl combine egg, milk, brown sugar, oil, and molasses. Add all at once to the dry mixture. Stir just till moistened (batter should be lumpy).

Spoon batter into the prepared muffin cups, filling each ⅔ full. Bake in a 400° oven about 20 minutes or till golden. Cool in muffin cups on a wire rack for 5 minutes. Remove muffins from muffin cups and place on a wire rack. Drizzle with Nutmeg Glaze, letting glaze drip down sides of muffins. Serve warm. Makes 12.

Nutmeg Glaze: In a small mixing bowl stir together ½ cup sifted *powdered sugar*, 2 teaspoons *rum* or *apple cider,* and ¼ teaspoon *ground nutmeg.* Mix till smooth. If necessary, add additional rum or apple cider to make of drizzling consistency.

Nutrition facts per muffin: 164 calories, 5 g total fat (1 g saturated fat), 19 mg cholesterol, 101 mg sodium, 26 g carbohydrate, 0 g fiber, 3 g protein.
Daily value: 1% vitamin A, 0% vitamin C, 7% calcium, 9% iron.

SPICED PUMPKIN MUFFINS

For a pleasant crunch, stir ⅓ cup finely chopped walnuts into the topping mixture before sprinkling over the batter.

2 cups all-purpose flour
½ cup sugar
2 teaspoons baking powder
1 teaspoon ground cinnamon
½ teaspoon ground nutmeg
¼ teaspoon salt
¼ teaspoon ground allspice
1 beaten egg
¾ cup milk
½ cup canned pumpkin
¼ cup cooking oil
  Crumb Topping

Grease twelve 2½-inch muffin cups. Set muffin cups aside.

In a medium mixing bowl stir together flour, sugar, baking powder, cinnamon, nutmeg, salt, and allspice. Make a well in the center of dry mixture.

In another medium mixing bowl combine egg, milk, pumpkin, and oil. Add all at once to the dry mixture. Stir just till moistened (batter should be lumpy).

Spoon batter into prepared muffin cups, filling each ⅔ full. Sprinkle with Crumb Topping. Bake in a 400° oven for 20 to 25 minutes or till golden. Cool in muffin cups on a wire rack for 5 minutes. Then remove muffins from muffin cups. Serve warm. Makes 12.

Crumb Topping: In a small mixing bowl combine ¼ cup packed *brown sugar*, ¼ cup *all-purpose flour*, and 2 tablespoons melted *butter* or *margarine*. Mix till crumbly.

Nutrition facts per muffin: 200 calories, 7 g total fat (2 g saturated fat), 24 mg cholesterol, 139 mg sodium, 30 g carbohydrate, 1 g fiber, 3 g protein.
Daily value: 26% vitamin A, 1% vitamin C, 7% calcium, 9% iron.

FIG MUFFINS

These cakelike muffins are chock full of chopped figs and pecans. Or try chopped dates and walnuts.

2   cups all-purpose flour
½   cup sugar
⅓   cup toasted wheat germ
2   teaspoons baking powder
½   teaspoon salt
¼   teaspoon baking soda
2   beaten eggs
¾   cup buttermilk
¼   cup cooking oil
1   cup chopped dried figs or dates
¼   cup finely chopped pecans, walnuts,
        or almonds (optional)

Grease twelve 2½-inch muffin cups or line with paper bake cups. Set muffin cups aside.

In a medium mixing bowl stir together flour, sugar, wheat germ, baking powder, salt, and baking soda. Make a well in the center of the dry mixture.

In another medium mixing bowl combine eggs, buttermilk, and oil. Add all at once to the dry mixture. Stir just till moistened (batter should be lumpy). Fold in figs or dates.

Spoon batter into the prepared muffin cups, filling each ⅔ full. Sprinkle with nuts, if desired. Bake in a 400° oven for 20 to 25 minutes or till golden. Cool in muffin cups on a wire rack for 5 minutes. Then remove muffins from muffin cups. Serve warm. Makes 12.

Nutrition facts per muffin: 215 calories, 6 g total fat (1 g saturated fat), 36 mg cholesterol, 205 mg sodium, 36 g carbohydrate, 2 g fiber, 5 g protein.
Daily value: 1% vitamin A, 0% vitamin C, 8% calcium, 11% iron.

OVERNIGHT DATE BRAN MUFFINS

Everyone likes freshly baked muffins for breakfast and with this recipe, you can mix them in advance. In the morning just bake and serve.

1¼ cups all-purpose flour
1 cup whole bran cereal
½ cup toasted wheat germ
½ cup sugar
1½ teaspoons baking powder
¼ teaspoon baking soda
¼ teaspoon salt
1 beaten egg
1½ cups buttermilk
¼ cup cooking oil
½ cup snipped pitted dates or raisins
½ cup chopped walnuts

In a large mixing bowl stir together flour, bran cereal, wheat germ, sugar, baking powder, baking soda, and salt. Make a well in the center of dry mixture.

In a medium mixing bowl combine egg, buttermilk, and oil. Add all at once to the dry mixture. Stir just till moistened (batter should be lumpy). Fold in dates or raisins and walnuts. Store in a covered container in the refrigerator at least 1 hour or up to 24 hours.

To bake muffins, gently stir batter. Grease desired number of 2½-inch muffin cups or line with paper bake cups. Spoon batter into the prepared muffin cups, filling each ⅔ full. Bake in a 400° oven about 20 minutes or till golden. Cool in muffin cups on a wire rack for 5 minutes. Then remove muffins from muffin cups. Serve warm. Makes about 16.

Nutrition facts per muffin: 159 calories, 7 g total fat (1 g saturated fat), 14 mg cholesterol, 145 mg sodium, 24 g carbohydrate, 2 g fiber, 4 g protein.
Daily value: *0% vitamin A, 7% vitamin C, 5% calcium, 10% iron.*

MARJORAM MUFFINS

Savory muffins like these complement most main dishes from soups to salads. Serve warm with creamy butter.

1¾ cup all-purpose flour
¼ cup sugar
2 teaspoons baking powder
2 teaspoons snipped fresh marjoram or
  ½ teaspoon dried marjoram, crushed
1 teaspoon snipped fresh rosemary or
  ¼ teaspoon dried rosemary, crushed
¼ teaspoon salt
1 beaten egg
¾ cup milk
¼ cup cooking oil

Grease twelve 2½-inch muffin cups or line with paper bake cups. Set muffin cups aside.

In a medium mixing bowl stir together flour, sugar, baking powder, marjoram, rosemary, and salt. Make a well in the center of the dry mixture.

In another medium mixing bowl combine egg, milk, and oil. Add all at once to the dry mixture. Stir just till moistened (batter should be lumpy).

Spoon batter into the prepared muffin cups, filling each ⅔ full. Bake in a 400° oven for 20 to 25 minutes or till golden. Cool in muffin cups on a wire rack for 5 minutes. Remove muffins from muffin cups. Serve warm. Makes 12.

Nutrition facts per muffin: 132 calories, 5 g total fat (1 g saturated fat), 19 mg cholesterol, 118 mg sodium, 18 g carbohydrate, 0 g fiber, 3 g protein.
Daily value: 1% vitamin A, 0% vitamin C, 6% calcium, 6% iron.

APPLE ALLSPICE BREAD

Like the other tea breads in this section, you'll find this bread slices best after 24 hours. Wrap the loaf in plastic wrap or foil before storing.

2   cups all-purpose flour
1   cup packed brown sugar
1½   teaspoons baking powder
¾   teaspoon ground allspice
½   teaspoon baking soda
¼   teaspoon salt
½   cup butter or margarine
2   beaten eggs
¼   cup milk
1   large Granny Smith or other baking
        apple (Rome, Golden Delicious)
        peeled, cored, and coarsely
        shredded (1 cup)
½   cup raisins or snipped pitted dates

Grease the bottom and ½ inch up the sides of a 9x5x3-inch loaf pan. Set aside.

In a large mixing bowl stir together flour, sugar, baking powder, allspice, baking soda, and salt. Using a pastry blender, cut in butter or margarine till mixture resembles coarse crumbs. Make a well in the center of crumb mixture.

In a medium mixing bowl beat together eggs and milk. Add shredded apple. Add egg mixture all at once to crumb mixture. Stir just till moistened (batter should be lumpy). Fold in raisins or dates.

Pour batter into loaf pan. Bake in a 350° oven for 60 to 65 minutes or till a wooden toothpick inserted near center comes out clean. (If necessary, cover with foil the last 10 to 15 minutes of baking to prevent overbrowning.) Cool in pan on a wire rack 10 minutes. Remove from pan and cool thoroughly on wire rack. Wrap and store overnight before slicing. Makes 1 loaf (16 servings).

Nutrition facts per serving: 175 calories, 7 g total fat (4 g saturated fat), 42 mg cholesterol, 179 mg sodium, 27 g carbohydrate, 1 g fiber, 3 g protein.
Daily value: 6% vitamin A, 0% vitamin C, 4% calcium, 7% iron.

SKILLET PEPPER CORN BREAD

If you like, omit the chili pepper and substitute Monterey Jack cheese with peppers for the cheddar cheese. You will save the step of chopping the fresh pepper.

1   cup cornmeal
½   cup all-purpose flour
2   teaspoons baking powder
¼   teaspoon salt
2   beaten eggs
½   cup milk
1   8¾-ounce can cream-style corn
2   tablespoons cooking oil
½   cup shredded cheddar cheese
1   fresh red or green jalapeño pepper,
      seeded and finely chopped

Spray an 8- or 9-inch cast-iron or oven-safe skillet with nonstick coating. Heat skillet in a 400° oven for 5 minutes just before filling.

In a large mixing bowl stir together cornmeal, flour, baking powder, and salt. Make a well in the center of dry mixture.

In a medium mixing bowl beat together eggs, milk, cream-style corn, and oil. Add egg mixture all at once to dry mixture. Stir just till moistened (batter should be lumpy). Fold in cheese and jalapeño pepper.

Pour batter into hot skillet. Bake for 20 to 25 minutes or till a wooden toothpick inserted near center comes out clean. Cool in skillet on wire rack 10 minutes. Serve warm. Makes 1 loaf (8 servings).

Nutrition facts per serving: 198 calories, 8 g total fat (3 g saturated fat), 62 mg cholesterol, 317 mg sodium, 26 g carbohydrate, 2 g fiber, 7 g protein.
Daily value: 6% vitamin A, 7% vitamin C, 13% calcium, 10% iron.

LEMON BREAD

Toasting the nuts for this tangy lemon bread intensifies their flavor. If you make two small loaves, you can freeze one for later.

½ cup butter
1 cup sugar
2 eggs
1⅔ cups all-purpose flour
¾ cup buttermilk
1½ teaspoons finely shredded lemon peel
½ teaspoon baking soda
¼ teaspoon salt
⅓ cup chopped almonds, walnuts, or
    pecans; toasted
    Lemon Glaze

Grease bottom and ½ inch up sides of one 8x4x2-inch loaf pan or two 7½x3½x2-inch loaf pans. Set aside.

In a large mixing bowl beat butter with an electric mixer on medium speed about 30 seconds or till softened. Add the sugar and beat about 5 minutes or till light and fluffy. Add eggs, one at a time, beating till combined. Add flour, buttermilk, lemon peel, baking soda, and salt. Beat just till combined. Stir in nuts.

Pour batter into prepared pan(s) and spread evenly. Bake in a 350° oven about 45 minutes for 8x4x2-inch loaf and about 40 minutes for 7½x3½x2-inch loaves or till a wooden toothpick inserted near center(s) comes out clean. (If necessary, cover loosely with foil for the last 10 to 15 minutes of baking to prevent overbrowning.)

Cool in pan(s) on wire rack 10 minutes. Remove from pan(s). Place on wire rack set over waxed paper.

Spoon Lemon Glaze over top(s). Cool completely on the wire rack. Wrap and store overnight before slicing. Makes 1 large loaf or 2 small loaves (16 servings).

Lemon Glaze: In a small mixing bowl stir together 3 tablespoons *lemon juice* and 1 tablespoon *sugar* till sugar is dissolved.

Nutrition facts per serving: 174 calories, 8 g total fat (4 g saturated fat), 42 mg cholesterol, 151 mg sodium, 24 g carbohydrate, 1 g fiber, 3 g protein.
Daily value: 6% vitamin A, 2% vitamin C, 2% calcium, 5% iron.

CARROT-ZUCCHINI LOAVES

The carrots and zucchini add a confettilike look to these moist loaves. Perfect served plain, or spread slices with a thin layer of whipped cream cheese.

2½ cups all-purpose flour
½ cup toasted wheat germ
2 teaspoons baking powder
½ teaspoon baking soda
½ teaspoon salt
3 beaten eggs
1 cup granulated sugar
1 cup finely shredded zucchini
1 cup finely shredded carrot
½ cup packed brown sugar
½ cup cooking oil

Grease bottom and ½ inch up sides of two 8x4x2-inch loaf pans. Set aside.

In a large mixing bowl stir together flour, wheat germ, baking powder, baking soda, and salt. Make a well in the center of dry mixture.

In a medium mixing bowl combine eggs, granulated sugar, zucchini, carrot, brown sugar, and oil and mix well. Add all at once to dry mixture. Stir just till moistened (batter should be lumpy).

Pour batter into loaf pans. Bake in a 350° oven for 45 to 55 minutes or till a wooden toothpick inserted near center comes out clean. (If necessary, cover loosely with foil during last 10 to 15 minutes of baking to prevent overbrowning.) Cool in pans on wire racks 10 minutes. Remove from pans and cool thoroughly on wire racks. Wrap and store overnight before slicing. Makes 2 loaves (24 servings).

Nutrition facts per serving: 151 calories, 6 g total fat (1 g saturated fat), 27 mg cholesterol, 112 mg sodium, 23 g carbohydrate, 1 g fiber, 3 g protein.
Daily value: 14% vitamin A, 1% vitamin C, 3% calcium, 6% iron.

BLUEBERRY ORANGE LOAF

To intensify the orange flavor, serve with an orange cream cheese spread. Make the spread by stirring 2 teaspoons finely shredded orange peel into 8 ounces softened cream cheese.

1 cup fresh or frozen blueberries, thawed
½ cup chopped pecans
1 tablespoon all-purpose flour
1 teaspoon finely shredded orange peel
3 cups all-purpose flour
1 cup sugar
1 tablespoon baking powder
½ teaspoon baking soda
½ teaspoon salt
1 beaten egg
1⅓ cups milk
¼ cup orange juice
¼ cup cooking oil
1 teaspoon vanilla

Grease bottom and ½ inch up sides of one 9x5x3-inch loaf pan or two 7½x3½x2-inch loaf pans. Set aside.

In a small mixing bowl combine blueberries, pecans, 1 tablespoon flour, and orange peel. Toss lightly to mix and set aside.

In a large mixing bowl stir together 3 cups flour, sugar, baking powder, baking soda, and salt. Make a well in the center of dry mixture.

In a medium mixing bowl combine egg, milk, orange juice, oil, and vanilla; mix well. Add all at once to dry mixture. Stir just till moistened (batter should be lumpy). Fold in blueberry mixture.

Pour batter into loaf pan(s). Bake in a 350° oven about 1 hour for 9x5x3-inch loaf or 45 to 50 minutes for 7½x3½x2-inch loaves or till a wooden toothpick inserted near center comes out clean. (If necessary, cover with foil the last 10 to 15 minutes of baking to prevent overbrowning.) Cool in pan(s) on wire rack(s) for 10 minutes. Remove from pan(s) and cool thoroughly on wire rack(s). Wrap and store overnight before slicing. Makes 2 small loaves or 1 large loaf (16 servings).

Nutrition facts per serving: 204 calories, 7 g total fat (1 g saturated fat), 15 mg cholesterol, 189 mg sodium, 33 g carbohydrate, 1 g fiber, 4 g protein.
Daily value: 2% vitamin A, 5% vitamin C, 7% calcium, 8% iron.

MAPLE PUMPKIN BREAD

You can substitute 2 teaspoons pumpkin pie spice for the spices in this fragrant, moist tea bread. Delicious served for an afternoon tea or with coffee for a quick breakfast.

2   cups all-purpose flour
2   teaspoons baking powder
1   teaspoon ground cinnamon
½   teaspoon baking soda
½   teaspoon ground nutmeg
½   teaspoon ground allspice
2   beaten eggs
1   cup packed brown sugar
1   cup canned pumpkin
½   cup maple syrup
⅓   cup cooking oil
1   cup chopped pecans
    Maple Glaze

Grease bottom and ½ inch up sides of a 9x5x3-inch loaf pan. Set pan aside.

In a large mixing bowl stir together flour, baking powder, cinnamon, baking soda, nutmeg, and allspice. Make a well in the center of dry mixture.

In a medium mixing bowl combine eggs, brown sugar, pumpkin, maple syrup, and oil and mix well. Add all at once to dry mixture. Stir just till moistened (batter should be lumpy). Fold in pecans.

Pour batter into loaf pan. Bake in a 350° oven for 60 to 65 minutes or till a wooden toothpick inserted near center comes out clean. (If necessary, cover with foil the last 10 to 15 minutes of baking to prevent overbrowning.) Cool in pan on a wire rack 10 minutes. Remove from pan and cool thoroughly on wire rack. Wrap and store overnight before slicing. Drizzle with Maple Glaze at least 1 hour before serving. Makes 1 loaf (16 servings).

Maple Glaze: In a small mixing bowl combine ½ cup sifted *powdered sugar* and 2 tablespoons *maple syrup.* If necessary, add *milk,* 1 teaspoon at a time, to make drizzling consistency.

Nutrition facts per serving: 238 calories, 10 g total fat (1 g saturated fat), 27 mg cholesterol, 98 mg sodium, 36 g carbohydrate, 1 g fiber, 3 g protein.
Daily value: 35% vitamin A, 1% vitamin C, 5% calcium, 10% iron.

CRUNCHY PARMESAN CORN BREAD

Flecks of sun-dried tomatoes and green onions give this bread both color and flavor. Serve warm with soup or salad.

1 cup boiling water
¼ cup bulgur
   Yellow cornmeal
1 cup all-purpose flour
1 cup yellow cornmeal
⅓ cup grated Parmesan cheese
2 tablespoons sugar
1 tablespoon baking powder
½ teaspoon fennel seed
½ teaspoon dried basil, crushed
2 beaten eggs
1 cup milk
¼ cup olive oil or cooking oil
⅓ cup sun-dried tomatoes (oil pack), drained and chopped, or diced pimiento, drained
⅓ cup sliced green onion

Pour boiling water over bulgur and let stand for 5 minutes. Drain. Meanwhile, grease bottom and ½ inch up sides of a 6-cup soufflé dish, an 8x4x2-inch loaf pan, or a 9x5x3-inch loaf pan. Sprinkle bottom and sides with cornmeal. Set aside.

In a large mixing bowl stir together flour, the 1 cup cornmeal, Parmesan cheese, sugar, baking powder, fennel seed, and basil. Make a well in the center of dry mixture.

In a medium mixing bowl combine eggs, milk, and oil. Stir in bulgur and mix well. Add all at once to dry mixture. Stir just till moistened (batter should be lumpy). Fold in tomatoes or pimiento and onion.

Pour batter into prepared dish or pan. Bake in a 375° oven for 50 to 55 minutes or till a wooden toothpick inserted near center comes out clean. (If necessary, cover loosely with foil for the last 10 to 15 minutes of baking to prevent overbrowning.) Remove from dish or pan. Cool on a wire rack for 30 minutes. Serve warm. Makes 1 loaf (8 servings).

Nutrition facts per serving: 269 calories, 11 g total fat (3 g saturated fat), 59 mg cholesterol, 259 mg sodium, 35 g carbohydrate, 2 g fiber, 8 g protein.
Daily value: *7% vitamin A, 9% vitamin C, 19% calcium, 13% iron.*

COTTAGE CHEESE CHIVE BISCUITS

These biscuits go well with any of your favorite comfort foods, such as homemade soups and stews.

    2   cups all-purpose flour
    2½ teaspoons baking powder
    ¼   teaspoon salt
    6   tablespoons butter or margarine
    ¾   cup small-curd cottage cheese
    ⅔   cup milk
    2   tablespoons snipped fresh chives or
            thinly sliced green onion tops

Line a baking sheet with foil; grease the foil. Set baking sheet aside.

In a medium mixing bowl stir together flour, baking powder, and salt. Using a pastry blender, cut in butter or margarine till mixture resembles coarse crumbs. Make a well in center of dry mixture. Add cottage cheese, milk, and chives all at once. Using a fork, stir just till moistened.

Drop dough by generous tablespoonfuls onto a greased foil-lined baking sheet. Bake in a 425° oven for 15 to 18 minutes or till golden. Remove biscuits from baking sheet and serve warm. Makes 12.

Nutrition facts per biscuit: 141 calories, 7 g total fat (4 g saturated fat), 18 mg cholesterol, 238 mg sodium, 16 g carbohydrate, 1 g fiber, 4 g protein.
Daily value: *6% vitamin A, 0% vitamin C, 8% calcium, 6% iron.*

ENGLISH TEA SCONES

Tender and slightly sweet, these treats are perfect for breakfast or afternoon tea. Serve with softly whipped and sweetened whipping cream.

2½ cups all-purpose flour
2 tablespoons sugar
4 teaspoons baking powder
¼ teaspoon salt
⅓ cup butter or margarine, cut into pieces
¾ cup whipping cream
2 beaten eggs
½ cup dried currants or snipped raisins
Milk
Sugar

In a medium mixing bowl stir together flour, 2 tablespoons sugar, baking powder, and salt. Using a pastry blender, cut in butter or margarine till mixture resembles coarse crumbs. Make a well in center of dry mixture. Add whipping cream, eggs, and currants or raisins all at once. Using a fork, stir just till moistened.

Turn dough out onto a lightly floured surface. Quickly knead dough by folding and pressing dough gently for 10 to 12 strokes or till dough is nearly smooth. Pat or lightly roll dough into an 8-inch square. Cut dough into 16 squares.

Place scones 1 inch apart on an ungreased baking sheet. Brush scones with milk and sprinkle with sugar. Bake in a 400° oven for 12 to 14 minutes or till golden. Remove scones from baking sheet and serve warm. Makes 16.

Nutrition facts per scone: 168 calories, 9 g total fat (5 g saturated fat), 52 mg cholesterol, 176 mg sodium, 20 g carbohydrate, 1 g fiber, 3 g protein.
Daily value: 9% vitamin A, 0% vitamin C, 8% calcium, 8% iron.

CHEDDAR CORNMEAL TWISTS

These savory biscuit sticks are filled with cheese and make the perfect accompaniment to a soup supper or a light salad lunch.

2 cups all-purpose flour
1 cup yellow cornmeal
2½ teaspoons baking powder
2 teaspoons sugar
½ teaspoon salt
½ cup shortening
1 cup milk
1 cup shredded sharp cheddar cheese
   (4 ounces)
   Paprika or ground red pepper

Grease a baking sheet; set aside.

In a large mixing bowl stir together flour, cornmeal, baking powder, sugar, and salt. Using a pastry blender, cut in shortening till mixture resembles coarse crumbs. Make a well in center of dry mixture. Add milk all at once. Using a fork, stir just till moistened.

Turn dough out onto a floured surface. Quickly knead dough by folding and pressing dough gently for 10 to 12 strokes or till dough is nearly smooth. Roll dough into a 15x8-inch rectangle. Sprinkle cheese lengthwise over half the dough. Fold dough in half lengthwise, covering the cheese. Pat edges of dough together to seal in cheese. Cut dough into twenty ¾-inch-wide strips. Sprinkle surface with paprika or ground red pepper. Holding a strip at both ends, carefully twist in opposite directions twice. Place on a greased baking sheet, pressing both ends down. Repeat with remaining strips.

Bake in a 450° oven for 8 to 10 minutes or till golden. Remove from baking sheet and serve warm. Makes 20.

Nutrition facts per twist: 143 calories, 7 g total fat (3 g saturated fat), 7 mg cholesterol, 140 mg sodium, 15 g carbohydrate, 1 g fiber, 4 g protein.
Daily value: 2% vitamin A, 0% vitamin C, 8% calcium, 6% iron.

ICED CHERRY SCONES

For a relaxing treat, serve hot tea with these warm-from-the-oven scones. Substitute currants for the dried cherries or raisins for a change of pace.

½ **cup snipped dried cherries or raisins**
2 **cups all-purpose flour**
3 **tablespoons brown sugar**
2 **teaspoons baking powder**
½ **teaspoon baking soda**
½ **teaspoon salt**
¼ **cup butter or margarine**
1 **teaspoon finely shredded orange peel**
1 **8-ounce carton dairy sour cream**
1 **beaten egg yolk**
   Orange Glaze

In a small mixing bowl pour enough boiling water over dried cherries or raisins to cover. Let stand for 5 minutes, then drain well.

In a large mixing bowl stir together flour, brown sugar, baking powder, baking soda, and salt. Using a pastry blender, cut in butter or margarine till mixture resembles coarse crumbs. Toss with drained cherries and orange peel. Make a well in center of dry mixture.

In a small bowl stir together sour cream and egg yolk. Add sour cream mixture all at once. Using a fork, stir just till moistened.

Turn dough onto a lightly floured surface. Quickly knead dough by folding and pressing dough gently for 10 to 12 strokes or till dough is nearly smooth. Pat or lightly roll dough into a 7-inch circle. Cut into 12 wedges.

Place wedges 1 inch apart on an ungreased baking sheet. Bake in a 400° oven for 10 to 12 minutes or till golden. Remove scones from baking sheet. Drizzle scones with Orange Glaze and serve warm. Makes 12.

Orange Glaze: In a small mixing bowl stir together 1 cup sifted *powdered sugar,* 1 tablespoon *orange juice,* and ¼ teaspoon *vanilla.* Stir in additional orange juice, 1 teaspoon at a time, till the glaze is of a drizzling consistency.

Nutrition facts per scone: 209 calories, 8 g total fat (5 g saturated fat), 36 mg cholesterol, 208 mg sodium, 31 g carbohydrate, 1 g fiber, 3 g protein.
Daily value: 13% vitamin A, 1% vitamin C, 7% calcium, 7% iron.

WALNUT SWIRLS

These lightly iced brown sugar-walnut rolls are fabulous with coffee or tea. They are a delectable quick-fix substitute for old-fashioned cinnamon yeast rolls.

1½ cups all-purpose flour
 ½ cup whole-wheat flour
 1 tablespoon baking powder
 2 teaspoons granulated sugar
 ½ teaspoon cream of tartar
 ¼ teaspoon salt
 ½ cup shortening
 ⅔ cup milk
 3 tablespoons butter or margarine,
     softened
 ½ cup packed brown sugar
 ⅓ cup chopped walnuts
 1 tablespoon all-purpose flour
 ½ cup sifted powdered sugar
 2 to 3 teaspoons milk

Grease an 11x7x2-inch or 9-inch round baking pan; set aside.

In a medium mixing bowl stir together 1½ cups all-purpose flour, whole-wheat flour, baking powder, sugar, cream of tartar, and salt. Using a pastry blender, cut in shortening till mixture resembles coarse crumbs. Make a well in center of dry mixture. Add ⅔ cup milk all at once. Using a fork, stir just till moistened.

Turn dough out onto a lightly floured surface. Quickly knead dough by folding and pressing dough gently for 10 to 12 strokes or till dough is nearly smooth. Lightly roll dough into a 12x8-inch rectangle. Spread with butter or margarine. Stir together brown sugar, walnuts, and 1 tablespoon all-purpose flour. Sprinkle dough with brown sugar mixture. Roll up dough, jelly-roll style, starting with one of the long sides. Slice dough into 12 pieces. Arrange slices, spiral-side up, in prepared pan. Bake in a 400° oven for 20 to 25 minutes or till golden.

Meanwhile, for icing, in a small mixing bowl combine powdered sugar with enough milk to make icing of drizzling consistency. Remove rolls from baking pan and place on a wire rack. Drizzle with icing and serve warm. Makes 12.

Nutrition facts per roll: 248 calories, 14 g total fat (4 g saturated fat), 9 mg cholesterol, 175 mg sodium, 29 g carbohydrate, 1 g fiber, 3 g protein.
Daily value: 3% vitamin A, 0% vitamin C, 9% calcium, 8% iron.

SWEET BISCUIT SHORTCAKES

Indulge in this all-time favorite dessert—plump juicy berries served on warm-from-the-oven biscuits and topped with sweetened whipped cream.

2¼ cups all-purpose flour
⅓ cup sugar
2 teaspoons baking powder
1½ teaspoons finely shredded orange peel
½ teaspoon salt
¼ teaspoon baking soda
½ cup butter or margarine
1 8-ounce carton dairy sour cream
⅓ cup milk
Milk
Pearl, coarse, or granulated sugar
4 cups mixed berries (raspberries, blueberries, and/or sliced strawberries)
2 tablespoons sugar
Sweetened Whipped Cream

In a medium mixing bowl stir together flour, ⅓ cup sugar, baking powder, orange peel, salt, and baking soda. Using a pastry blender, cut in butter or margarine till mixture resembles coarse crumbs. Make a well in center of dry mixture. Add sour cream and ⅓ cup milk all at once. Using a fork, stir just till moistened.

Turn dough out onto a lightly floured surface. Quickly knead dough by folding and pressing gently for 10 to 12 strokes or till dough is nearly smooth. Pat or lightly roll dough to ½-inch thickness. Cut dough with a floured 2½-inch round cutter. Place rounds on an ungreased baking sheet. Brush rounds with milk. Sprinkle with pearl, coarse, or granulated sugar. Bake in a 425° oven for 15 to 18 minutes or till golden.

Meanwhile, toss together berries and 2 tablespoons sugar. Remove shortcakes from baking sheet and split horizontally into halves. Serve warm or cooled shortcakes with berries and Sweetened Whipped Cream. Makes 8 servings.

Sweetened Whipped Cream: In a chilled medium mixing bowl combine 1 cup *whipping cream,* 2 tablespoons *sugar,* and 1 teaspoon *vanilla.* Beat with an electric mixer on medium to high speed till soft peaks form.

Nutrition facts per serving: 357 calories, 16 g total fat (10 g saturated fat), 43 mg cholesterol, 399 mg sodium, 49 g carbohydrate, 3 g fiber, 5 g protein.
Daily value: 15% vitamin A, 49% vitamin C, 12% calcium, 13% iron.

GINGERBREAD SCONES

Richer and more tender than its cousin the biscuit, scones usually contain eggs. This one retains all the richness without the egg.

2¼	cups all-purpose flour
1	tablespoon sugar
2½	teaspoons baking powder
1	teaspoon ground cinnamon
1	teaspoon ground ginger
¼	teaspoon baking soda
¼	teaspoon salt
⅔	cup butter or margarine
½	cup buttermilk
¼	cup molasses
¼	cup finely chopped candied ginger
	Milk
	Coarse or granulated sugar

In a medium mixing bowl stir together flour, 1 tablespoon sugar, baking powder, cinnamon, ground ginger, baking soda, and salt. Using a pastry blender, cut in butter or margarine till mixture resembles coarse crumbs. Make a well in center of dry mixture.

In a small mixing bowl stir together the buttermilk, molasses, and candied ginger. Add buttermilk mixture all at once to dry mixture. Using a fork, stir just till moistened.

Turn dough out onto a lightly floured surface. Quickly knead dough by folding and pressing dough gently for 10 to 12 strokes or till dough is nearly smooth. Pat or lightly roll dough into an 8-inch circle. Cut into 12 wedges.

Place wedges 1 inch apart on an ungreased baking sheet. Brush with milk and sprinkle with coarse or granulated sugar. Bake in a 400° oven about 15 minutes or till bottoms are brown. Remove scones from baking sheet and serve warm. Makes 12.

Nutrition facts per scone: 212 calories, 11 g total fat (6 g saturated fat), 28 mg cholesterol, 262 mg sodium, 27 g carbohydrate, 1 g fiber, 3 g protein.
Daily value: 9% vitamin A, 0% vitamin C, 8% calcium, 10% iron.

IRISH SODA BREAD

So simple, yet satisfying, this traditional bread is ready to serve in no time and tastes best with a little softened butter or margarine.

1 cup whole wheat flour
1 cup all-purpose flour
1 teaspoon baking powder
½ teaspoon baking soda
¼ teaspoon salt
3 tablespoons butter or margarine
1 beaten egg
¾ cup buttermilk
2 tablespoons brown sugar
⅓ cup dried cherries, dried cranberries, or raisins
1 beaten egg

In a medium mixing bowl stir together whole wheat flour, all-purpose flour, baking powder, baking soda, and salt. Using a pastry blender, cut in butter or margarine till mixture resembles coarse crumbs. Make a well in center of dry mixture. Add 1 egg; buttermilk; brown sugar; and cherries, cranberries, or raisins all at once. Using a fork, stir just till moistened.

Turn dough out onto a lightly floured surface. Quickly knead dough by folding and pressing dough gently for 10 to 12 strokes or till dough is nearly smooth. Shape dough into a 6-inch round loaf. Cut a 4-inch cross, ½ inch deep, on the top.

Place loaf on prepared baking sheet. Brush with remaining egg. Bake in a 375° oven about 35 minutes or till golden. Remove from baking sheet and serve warm. Makes 1 loaf (8 servings).

Nutrition facts per serving: 196 calories, 6 g total fat (3 g saturated fat), 66 mg cholesterol, 276 mg sodium, 30 g carbohydrate, 3 g fiber, 6 g protein.
Daily value: *9% vitamin A, 0% vitamin C, 7% calcium, 10% iron.*

LEMON PEPPER BISCUIT STICKS

These nicely seasoned biscuits are the perfect choice for your favorite main dishes. The lemon pepper seasoning gives them a flavor kick.

2   cups all-purpose flour
2   tablespoons sugar
2   teaspoons baking powder
1   teaspoon lemon pepper seasoning
¼   teaspoon baking soda
6   tablespoons butter or margarine
1   beaten egg
⅓   cup buttermilk
     Lemon pepper seasoning (optional)

In a medium mixing bowl stir together flour, sugar, baking powder, 1 teaspoon lemon pepper seasoning, and baking soda. Using a pastry blender, cut in butter or margarine till mixture resembles coarse crumbs. Make a well in center of dry mixture. Add egg and buttermilk all at once. Using a fork, stir just till moistened.

Turn dough out onto a lightly floured surface. Quickly knead dough by folding and pressing dough gently for 10 to 12 strokes or till dough is nearly smooth. Lightly roll dough into a 12x6-inch rectangle. Cut dough into twenty-four 6-inch strips.

Place strips ½ inch apart on an ungreased baking sheet. If desired, sprinkle with additional lemon pepper seasoning. Bake in a 400° oven for 10 to 12 minutes or till golden. Cool on baking sheet on wire rack 10 minutes. Remove from baking sheet and cool on rack. Makes 24.

Nutrition facts per stick: 69 calories, 3 g total fat (2 g saturated fat), 17 mg cholesterol, 124 mg sodium, 9 g carbohydrate, 0 g fiber, 1 g protein.
Daily value: 3% vitamin A, 0% vitamin C, 2% calcium, 3% iron.

SWEET POTATO BISCUITS

Choose these thyme-scented biscuits for dinner or lunch. Delightful with roast turkey, fried chicken, and glazed ham as well as pork roast and chops.

2 **cups all-purpose flour**
2 **teaspoons snipped fresh thyme or**
      ½ teaspoon dried thyme, crushed
2 **teaspoons baking powder**
½ **teaspoon baking soda**
½ **teaspoon salt**
¼ **cup shortening**
1 **cup mashed cooked sweet potatoes or**
      mashed canned sweet potatoes
½ **cup milk**
2 **tablespoons brown sugar**

In a medium mixing bowl stir together flour, thyme, baking powder, baking soda, and salt. Using a pastry blender, cut in shortening till mixture resembles coarse crumbs.

In another medium mixing bowl stir together sweet potatoes, milk, and brown sugar. Make a well in center of dry mixture. Add sweet potato mixture all at once. Using a fork, stir just till moistened.

Turn dough out onto a lightly floured surface. Quickly knead dough by folding and pressing dough gently for 10 to 12 strokes or till dough is nearly smooth. Pat or lightly roll dough to ½-inch thickness. Cut dough with a floured 2½-inch round cutter, dipping cutter into flour between cuts.

Place biscuits 1 inch apart on an ungreased baking sheet. Bake in a 425° oven for 12 to 15 minutes or till golden. Remove biscuits from baking sheet and serve warm. Makes 12.

Nutrition facts per biscuit: 149 calories, 5 g total fat (1 g saturated fat), 1 mg cholesterol, 211 mg sodium, 24 g carbohydrate, 1 g fiber, 3 g protein.
Daily value: 47% vitamin A, 7% vitamin C, 6% calcium, 8% iron.

GOAT CHEESE & ONION SCONES

These flaky wedges also taste great when made with crumbled feta cheese and 1 tablespoon snipped chives.

2   cups all-purpose flour
1   green onion, finely chopped
2   teaspoons baking powder
¼   teaspoon baking soda
¼   teaspoon salt
¼   teaspoon freshly ground pepper
4   ounces semi-soft goat cheese (chèvre),
       crumbled or cut into small cubes
½   cup buttermilk
1   beaten egg

In a medium mixing bowl stir together flour, green onion, baking powder, baking soda, salt, and pepper. Make a well in center of dry mixture. Add cheese, buttermilk, and egg. Using a fork, stir just till moistened.

Turn dough out onto a lightly floured surface. Quickly knead dough by folding and pressing dough gently for 10 to 12 strokes or till dough is nearly smooth. Divide dough in half. Pat or lightly roll half of the dough into a 5-inch round. Cut into 6 wedges. Repeat with remaining dough.

Place scones 1 inch apart on an ungreased baking sheet. Bake in a 400° oven for 15 to 18 minutes or till golden. Remove scones from baking sheet and serve warm. Makes 12.

Nutrition facts per scone: 112 calories, 3 g total fat (2 g saturated fat), 27 mg cholesterol, 203 mg sodium, 15 g carbohydrate, 1 g fiber, 5 g protein.
Daily value: 2% vitamin A, 0% vitamin C, 6% calcium, 7% iron.

PARMESAN CHEESE CRESCENTS

These light and flaky rolls are a snap to make and add a homemade touch to any meal.

2¼ cups all-purpose flour
 2 teaspoons baking powder
 ½ teaspoon salt
 ¼ teaspoon baking soda
 ½ cup shortening
 ¾ cup buttermilk
 1 tablespoon butter or margarine,
      melted
 ⅓ cup grated Parmesan cheese
 2 tablespoons finely snipped fresh
      parsley
     Milk
     Grated Parmesan cheese

In a medium mixing bowl stir together flour, baking powder, salt, and baking soda. Using a pastry blender, cut in shortening till mixture resembles coarse crumbs. Make a well in center of dry mixture, then add buttermilk all at once. Using a fork, stir just till moistened.

Turn dough out onto a lightly floured surface. Quickly knead dough by folding and pressing dough gently for 10 to 12 strokes or till dough is nearly smooth. Roll dough into 13-inch circle. Brush with melted butter or margarine. Sprinkle with ⅓ cup Parmesan cheese and the parsley. Cut into 12 wedges. Roll up each wedge from the wide end to the point.

Place crescents seam side down about 2 inches apart on an ungreased baking sheet, curving to form crescents. Brush with milk and sprinkle with additional Parmesan cheese. Bake in a 425° oven for 15 to 20 minutes or till golden. Remove crescents from baking sheet and serve warm. Makes 12.

Nutrition facts per crescent: 185 calories, 11 g total fat (3 g saturated fat), 6 mg cholesterol, 264 mg sodium, 18 g carbohydrate, 1 g fiber, 4 g protein.
Daily value: 2% vitamin A, 1% vitamin C, 10% calcium, 7% iron.

BERRY CORNMEAL SCONES

Scones usually taste best when served warm and crusty with softened butter or cream cheese.

1¼ cups all-purpose flour
 ¾ cup cornmeal
 ¼ cup sugar
 2 teaspoons baking powder
 ¼ teaspoon baking soda
 ¼ teaspoon salt
 ⅓ cup butter or margarine
 1 teaspoon finely shredded lemon peel
 ⅔ cup buttermilk
 1 cup fresh or frozen blueberries or
      raspberries, thawed
 1 teaspoon vanilla

In a medium mixing bowl stir together flour, cornmeal, sugar, baking powder, baking soda, and salt. Using a pastry blender, cut in butter or margarine till mixture resembles coarse crumbs. Add lemon peel. Make a well in center of dry mixture, then add buttermilk, berries, and vanilla all at once. Using a fork, stir just till moistened.

Turn dough out onto a lightly floured surface. Quickly knead dough by folding and pressing dough gently for 10 to 12 strokes or till dough is nearly smooth. Pat or lightly roll dough into an 8-inch circle on an ungreased baking sheet. Cut dough into 10 wedges, cutting only about halfway through dough to score.

Bake in a 400° oven for 20 to 25 minutes or till golden. Cut into wedges and remove scones from baking sheet. Serve warm. Makes 10.

Nutrition facts per scone: 180 calories, 7 g total fat (4 g saturated fat), 17 mg cholesterol, 238 mg sodium, 27 g carbohydrate, 1 g fiber, 3 g protein.
Daily value: *6% vitamin A, 3% vitamin C, 7% calcium, 8% iron.*

CRUMB-TOPPED APPLE KUCHEN

Kuchens originated in Germany, but are now enjoyed throughout Europe and the U.S. Serve this sweet coffee cake for breakfast or for dessert.

2½ cups all-purpose flour
1 package active dry yeast
½ cup milk
⅓ cup sugar
⅓ cup butter or margarine
½ teaspoon salt
2 eggs
3 large baking apples, pared, cored, and sliced
2 teaspoons lemon juice
   Crumb Topping
   Lemon Icing

In a large mixing bowl stir together *1 cup* of the flour and the yeast. In a medium saucepan heat and stir milk, sugar, butter or margarine, and salt just till warm (120° to 130°) and butter almost melts. Add milk mixture to flour mixture. Add eggs. Beat with an electric mixer on low to medium speed for 30 seconds, scraping the sides of the bowl constantly. Then beat on high speed for 3 minutes. Using a wooden spoon, stir in remaining flour (batter will be stiff).

Divide dough in half. With rubber spatula, spread evenly into two greased 8x1½ -inch round baking pans. Toss apple slices with lemon juice. Arrange apple slices on top of the batter. Top with Crumb Topping. Cover and let rise in a warm place till nearly double (45 to 50 minutes).

Bake in a 375° oven about 30 minutes or till apples are tender and a toothpick inserted into dough comes out clean. Cool in pans on wire racks for 10 minutes. Drizzle with Lemon Icing. Serve warm or cold. Makes 2 kuchens (12 servings).

Crumb Topping: In small bowl combine ¾ cup packed *brown sugar*, ⅓ cup *all-purpose flour*, 3 tablespoons *butter* or *margarine*, and 1 teaspoon *ground cinnamon*. Mix till crumbly.

Lemon Icing: In a small bowl combine 1 cup *powdered sugar* and 1 tablespoon *lemon juice*. Add 2 to 3 teaspoons *water* to make drizzling consistency. Mix till smooth.

Nutrition facts per serving: 299 calories, 9 g total fat (5 g saturated fat), 58 mg cholesterol, 189 mg sodium, 51 g carbohydrate, 1 g fiber, 5 g protein.
Daily value: 9% vitamin A, 3% vitamin C, 3% calcium, 12% iron.

ORANGE SAVARIN RING

Savarin is a festive French yeast cake soaked in spirits and served as a dessert. We eliminated the liquor in this version and drizzled it with orange marmalade and orange-flavored syrup.

1 package active dry yeast
1 teaspoon sugar
½ cup warm water (105° to 115°)
½ cup butter, softened
¼ cup sugar
½ teaspoon salt
2 eggs
1¾ cups all-purpose flour
1 tablespoon finely shredded
    orange peel
  Orange Syrup
¾ cup orange marmalade, warmed
3 cups fresh fruit (strawberries,
    raspberries, blueberries, and/or
    sliced kiwi fruit)
  Sweetened Whipped Cream
    (see recipe, page 71)

In a small mixing bowl sprinkle yeast and 1 teaspoon sugar over warm water. Stir to soften. Let stand 5 minutes or until foamy.

In a large mixing bowl stir together butter, ¼ cup sugar, and salt. Beat with an electric mixer on medium speed till fluffy. Add eggs, one at a time, beating well after each addition. Add yeast mixture. Add flour and beat on low speed till blended. Then beat on medium speed for 2 minutes. Stir in orange peel. Spoon dough into well-greased 6½-cup ring mold. Cover and let rise in a warm place till nearly double (for 45 to 60 minutes).

Bake in a 350° oven about 35 minutes or till a wooden toothpick inserted in center comes out clean. Cool in pan on rack 5 minutes. Loosen edge and turn out on a wire rack placed over a tray. Prick warm ring in several places with a long-tined fork. Slowly spoon Orange Syrup over warm ring till all is absorbed. Drizzle with warmed orange marmalade. Cool. Fill center of ring with fresh fruit and top with sweetened whipped cream, if desired. Makes 1 coffee cake (12 servings).

Orange Syrup: In small saucepan combine ½ cup *orange juice*, ½ cup *water*, and ½ cup *sugar*. Bring to boiling over medium-high heat, stirring till sugar is dissolved. Remove from heat.

Nutrition facts per serving: 261 calories, 9 g total fat (5 g saturated fat), 56 mg cholesterol, 181 mg sodium, 44 g carbohydrate, 3 g fiber, 4 g protein.
Daily value: 9% vitamin A, 35% vitamin C, 2% calcium, 8% iron.

PEANUT BUTTER & JELLY COFFEE CAKES

Perfect for a quick breakfast treat with a glass of milk—especially on a cold wintry morning.

2   cups all-purpose flour
¾   cup packed brown sugar
2   teaspoons baking powder
¼   teaspoon baking soda
¼   teaspoon salt
1   cup milk
½   cup peanut butter
2   eggs
¼   cup butter or margarine, softened
1   cup strawberry or grape jelly
    Crumb Topping

In a large mixing bowl stir together flour, brown sugar, baking powder, baking soda, and salt. Add milk, peanut butter, eggs, and butter or margarine. Beat with an electric mixer on low speed till mixed. Then beat on medium speed for 1 minute, scraping the sides of the bowl constantly.

Spread about *two-thirds* of the batter into a greased 13x9x2-inch baking pan. Stir jelly and spoon over batter. Drop remaining batter in small mounds on top of the jelly. Sprinkle with Crumb Topping. Bake in a 350° oven for 30 to 35 minutes or till golden brown. Serve warm. Makes 1 coffee cake (12 servings).

Crumb Topping: In a small mixing bowl stir together ½ cup packed *brown sugar* and ½ cup *all-purpose flour.* Cut in ¼ cup *peanut butter* and 3 tablespoons *butter* or *margarine* till crumbly.

Nutrition facts per serving: 400 calories, 16 g total fat (6 g saturated fat), 55 mg cholesterol, 306 mg sodium, 58 g carbohydrate, 2 g fiber, 8 g protein. Daily value: 9% vitamin A, 1% vitamin C, 9% calcium, 15% iron.

ALMOND TWISTS

The winning combination of almond and chocolate will please both guests and family.

4¼ to 4¾ cups all-purpose flour
  1 package quick-rising active dry yeast
  1 cup milk
  ⅓ cup sugar
  ⅓ cup butter or margarine
  1 teaspoon salt
  2 eggs
  1 12½-ounce can almond cake and
       pastry filling
  ½ cup miniature semisweet chocolate
       pieces

In a large mixing bowl stir together *2 cups* of the flour and the yeast. In a saucepan heat and stir milk, sugar, butter, and salt just till warm (120° to 130°). Add to flour mixture. Add eggs. Beat on low speed for 30 seconds, scraping the sides of the bowl. Beat on high speed for 3 minutes. Stir in as much of the remaining flour as you can.

On a lightly floured surface, knead in remaining flour to make a moderately soft dough (6 to 8 minutes). Shape the dough into a ball. Place dough in a lightly greased bowl, turning once to grease surface of the dough. Cover and let dough rest about 20 minutes. Punch dough down and turn out on a lightly floured surface. Divide dough in half. Roll half of the dough into a 24x8-inch rectangle. Spread with *half* of the almond filling and *2 tablespoons* of the chocolate pieces.

Fold dough loosely from one of the short sides, making about eight 3-inch-wide folds. (This is similar to rolling a jelly roll except you fold the dough instead of rolling it.) Place on a greased baking sheet. Make 2-inch-long cuts into the dough at ¾-inch intervals on one of the long sides. (Do not cut completely through to the other long side of dough roll.) Flip every other cut to the opposite side. Twist each cut in the same direction to expose the filling. Repeat, making a second loaf with the remaining dough. Cover loaves and let rise in a warm place till nearly double (about 30 minutes).

Bake in a 375° oven for 18 to 20 minutes or till golden, covering with foil after 10 minutes to prevent overbrowning. Sprinkle each loaf with half of the remaining chocolate pieces while the loaf is still warm. Serve warm. Makes 2 loaves (20 servings).

Nutrition facts per serving: 222 calories, 7 g total fat (2 g saturated fat), 30 mg cholesterol, 173 mg sodium, 37 g carbohydrate, 2 g fiber, 4 g protein.
Daily value: 4% vitamin A, 0% vitamin C, 1% calcium, 11% iron.

EASY CRUMB COFFEE CAKE

Tender, moist, and exceptionally good, this coffee cake is simple to make because both the topping and the cake start with the same crumb base.

1¾ cups all-purpose flour
1 cup sugar
1 teaspoon ground cinnamon
½ cup butter or margarine
2 teaspoons baking powder
½ teaspoon salt
1 egg
½ cup milk
1 teaspoon vanilla
 Sifted powdered sugar

In a medium mixing bowl stir together flour, sugar, and cinnamon. Using a pastry blender, cut in butter or margarine till mixture resembles coarse crumbs. Remove *½ cup* crumb mixture and set aside.

Add baking powder and salt to remaining crumb mixture. Make a well in center of dry mixture. Then add egg, milk, and vanilla all at once. Using a fork, stir just till moistened.

Pour batter into greased 8x8x2-inch square baking pan. Sprinkle reserved crumb mixture over batter.

Bake in a 375° oven for 35 to 40 minutes or till golden brown and a wooden toothpick inserted in center comes out clean. Cool in pan on a wire rack. Serve warm or cold. Sift powdered sugar over the top of the cake. Makes 1 coffee cake (9 servings).

Nutrition facts per serving: 274 calories, 11 g total fat (7 g saturated fat), 52 mg cholesterol, 317 mg sodium, 41 g carbohydrate, 1 g fiber, 4 g protein.
Daily value: 11% vitamin A, 0% vitamin C, 8% calcium, 9% iron.

CHOCOLATE BRAID

This mildly flavored chocolate yeast bread is special enough for dessert. It's quite attractive, too, with its drizzle of vanilla icing and sprinkled toasted almonds.

5¼ to 5¾ cups all-purpose flour
2 packages active dry yeast
½ cup unsweetened cocoa powder
⅓ cup instant mashed potato flakes
1 teaspoon instant coffee crystals
2 cups milk
⅓ cup sugar
¼ cup butter or margarine
1 teaspoon salt
2 eggs
Vanilla Icing
Toasted sliced almonds (optional)

In a large mixing bowl stir together *2 cups* of the flour, yeast, cocoa, potato flakes, and coffee crystals. In a saucepan heat and stir milk, sugar, butter, and salt just till warm (120° to 130°). Add to flour mixture. Add eggs. Beat on low speed for 30 seconds, scraping the sides of the bowl. Beat on high speed for 3 minutes. Stir in as much of the remaining flour as you can.

On a lightly floured surface, knead in the remaining flour to make a moderately soft dough (6 to 8 minutes total). Place dough in a lightly greased bowl, turning once to grease surface of the dough. Cover and let rise in a warm place till double (about 1 hour).

Punch dough down on a floured surface. Cover and let rest for 10 minutes. Divide dough into six portions. Grease two baking sheets. Roll each portion of the dough into a ball. Roll each ball into a thick rope about 16 inches long. Line up three of the ropes, 1 inch apart, on a baking sheet. Braid by bringing left rope underneath center rope. Bring right rope under new center rope. Repeat to end. (Braid the ropes loosely so the bread has room to expand.) Press rope ends together to seal. Repeat braiding with remaining three ropes. Cover and let rise in a warm place till double (for 30 to 40 minutes). Bake in a 350° oven for 30 to 35 minutes or till done. Remove from baking sheets. Cool on wire racks. Drizzle with Vanilla Icing. Sprinkle with toasted almonds, if desired. Makes 2 loaves (32 servings).

Vanilla Icing: In small mixing bowl stir together 2 cups sifted *powdered sugar*, 2 tablespoons *milk*, and ¼ teaspoon *vanilla flavoring*. Stir till smooth, adding more *milk*, 1 teaspoon at a time, to make drizzling consistency.

Nutrition facts per serving: 139 calories, 3 g total fat (1 g saturated fat), 18 mg cholesterol, 94 mg sodium, 25 g carbohydrate, 1 g fiber, 4 g protein.
Daily value: 2% vitamin A, 0% vitamin C, 3% calcium, 8% iron.

BLUEBERRY CRUMB COFFEE CAKE

Blueberries add a sweet touch to this tender-crumbed coffee cake. You can store it in the freezer for a special brunch. Warm and serve.

⅓ cup butter or margarine
⅔ cup sugar
2 eggs
2 cups all-purpose flour
⅓ cup milk
2 teaspoons baking powder
½ teaspoon salt
2 cups fresh or frozen blueberries,
    thawed
   Cinnamon Crumbs

In a large mixing bowl beat butter or margarine with an electric mixer on medium speed about 30 seconds or till softened. Add sugar and beat about 3 minutes or till light and fluffy. Add eggs, one at a time, beating till combined. Add flour, milk, baking powder, and salt. Beat just till moistened. Fold in blueberries.

Pour batter into a greased 8- or 9-inch square baking pan. Sprinkle with Cinnamon Crumbs. Bake in a 375° oven for 35 to 40 minutes or till a wooden toothpick inserted near center comes out clean.

Cool in pan on wire rack 10 minutes. Serve warm or at room temperature. Makes 1 coffee cake (9 servings).

Cinnamon Crumbs: In a medium mixing bowl combine ½ cup packed *brown sugar*, ¼ cup *all-purpose flour*, 1 teaspoon *ground cinnamon*, and ¼ cup softened *butter* or *margarine*. Mix with a fork till crumbly.

Nutrition facts per serving: 343 calories, 14 g total fat (8 g saturated fat), 80 mg cholesterol, 344 mg sodium, 52 g carbohydrate, 2 g fiber, 5 g protein.
Daily value: 13% vitamin A, 7% vitamin C, 9% calcium, 13% iron.

OVERNIGHT BUBBLE LOAF

This yeast loaf is a great choice for a make-ahead bread. It waits in the refrigerator, shaped and ready to bake.

3½ to 4 cups all-purpose flour
 1 package active dry yeast
1⅓ cups milk
 2 tablespoons honey
 1 tablespoon butter or margarine
 ¾ teaspoon salt
 1 egg
 ⅔ cup toasted wheat germ
 ¼ cup butter or margarine
 ⅔ cup packed brown sugar
 3 tablespoons light corn syrup
 ½ teaspoon ground cinnamon
 ⅓ cup chopped walnuts
 3 tablespoons butter or margarine,
    melted
 ⅓ cup granulated sugar
 1 teaspoon ground cinnamon

In a mixing bowl stir together *1½ cups* flour and yeast. In a saucepan heat and stir milk, honey, 1 tablespoon butter, and salt just till warm (120° to 130°). Add milk mixture to flour mixture. Add egg. Beat with an electirc mixer on low speed for 30 seconds, scraping the sides of the bowl. Beat on high speed for 3 minutes. Stir in wheat germ and as much of the remaining flour as you can.

On a lightly floured surface, knead in enough of the remaining flour to make a moderately soft dough that is smooth and elastic (3 to 5 minutes total). Place dough in a lightly greased bowl, turning once to grease surface of dough. Cover and let rest 20 minutes. Meanwhile, in a saucepan heat ¼ cup butter, brown sugar, corn syrup, and ½ teaspoon cinnamon, stirring till smooth. Set aside.

Divide dough into 4 portions. Divide each portion into 4 pieces (16 pieces total). Roll each piece into a ball. Place walnuts in bottom of greased 10-inch fluted tube pan. Dip dough balls in 3 tablespoons melted butter and coat with mixture of ⅓ cup granulated sugar and cinnamon. Place half of the coated dough balls in a single layer in prepared pan. Drizzle with about *one-third* of the brown sugar mixture. Top with remaining coated dough balls and drizzle with remaining brown sugar mixture. Cover lightly with oiled waxed paper, then plastic wrap, and chill for 2 to 24 hours.

Uncover. Let stand about 20 minutes. Bake in a 350° oven for 35 to 40 minutes or till bread sounds hollow when tapped. Cool in pan on a wire rack for 5 minutes. Turn bread onto serving platter. Cool about 45 minutes and serve. Makes 1 coffee cake (16 servings).

Nutrition facts per serving: 256 calories, 9 g total fat (4 g saturated fat), 30 mg cholesterol, 178 mg sodium, 40 g carbohydrate, 1 g fiber, 6 g protein.
Daily value: 7% vitamin A, 1% vitamin C, 3% calcium, 14% iron.

RASPBERRY ALMOND COFFEE CAKE

One of our recipe testers called this a simply lovely coffee cake. It's moist, tender, too, and pretty as a picture.

1   **cup all-purpose flour**
¼   **cup sugar**
1   **teaspoon baking powder**
¼   **teaspoon baking soda**
¼   **teaspoon salt**
1   **beaten egg**
½   **cup dairy sour cream**
¼   **cup butter or margarine, melted**
1   **cup fresh or frozen lightly sweetened
     raspberries**
2   **tablespoons brown sugar**
⅓   **cup sliced almonds
     Almond Icing**

Grease bottom and sides of an 8x1½-inch round baking pan.

In a large mixing bowl stir together flour, granulated sugar, baking powder, baking soda, and salt. Make a well in center of dry mixture.

In another bowl beat together egg, sour cream, and butter or margarine. Add egg mixture all at once to dry mixture. Stir just till moistened (and batter is lumpy).

Spread *two-thirds* of batter into prepared baking pan. Sprinkle with raspberries and brown sugar. Drop remaining batter by spoonfuls on top. Sprinkle with almonds. Bake in a 350° oven for 30 to 35 minutes or till a wooden toothpick inserted near center comes out clean.

Cool in pan on wire rack 10 minutes. Remove from pan, if desired. Cool about 20 minutes more. Drizzle with Almond Icing. Serve warm or at room temperature. Makes 1 coffee cake (8 servings).

Almond Icing: In a small mixing bowl combine ½ cup sifted *powdered sugar*, 1 teaspoon *milk*, and ¼ teaspoon *almond flavoring*. Stir till smooth. Add additional milk (½ to 1 teaspoon) to make drizzling consistency.

Nutrition facts per serving: 235 calories, 12 g total fat (6 g saturated fat), 48 mg cholesterol, 227 mg sodium, 30 g carbohydrate, 2 g fiber, 4 g protein.
Daily value: 10% vitamin A, 6% vitamin C, 7% calcium, 8% iron.

WELSH-RAREBIT BREAD

This full-flavored cheesy bread has an even texture, flecked throughout with sun-dried tomatoes. It's delicious toasted, too.

4¾ to 5¼ cups all-purpose flour
  2 packages active dry yeast
  1 teaspoon dry mustard
1¾ cups milk
  2 tablespoons sugar
  1 tablespoon butter or margarine
  1 teaspoon salt
  ¼ teaspoon cayenne pepper
  2 tablespoons Worcestershire sauce
  2 cups shredded sharp cheddar cheese
      (8 ounces)
  ½ cup sun-dried tomatoes (packed in
      oil), drained and snipped
      Cooking oil

In a mixing bowl stir together *2 cups* of flour, yeast, and mustard. In a saucepan heat and stir milk, sugar, butter, salt, and pepper just till warm (120° to 130°). Add milk mixture to flour mixture. Add Worcestershire sauce. Beat on low speed for 30 seconds, scraping the sides of the bowl. Beat on high speed for 3 minutes. Add cheese and tomatoes. Stir in as much of the remaining flour as you can.

On a lightly floured surface, knead in enough of the remaining flour to make a moderately soft dough that is smooth and elastic (8 to 10 minutes total). Shape the dough into a ball. Place dough in a lightly greased bowl, turning once to grease surface of the dough. Cover and let rise in a warm place till double (about 1 hour).

Punch dough down. Turn dough out onto a lightly floured surface. Divide dough in half. Cover and let rest for 10 minutes. Meanwhile, lightly grease two 9x5x3-inch or 8x4x2-inch loaf pans.

Shape each portion of the dough into a braid by rolling it into a 10x6-inch rectangle. Cut into three 10-inch strips. Form into ropes. Stretch each to 15-inch length. Braid together, tucking ends under. Place the braids in the prepared pans. Brush lightly with oil. Cover and let rise in a warm place till nearly double (for 30 to 40 minutes).

Bake in a 350° oven for 35 to 45 minutes or till bread sounds hollow when you tap the top with your fingers. Immediately remove bread from pans. Cool on wire racks. Makes 2 loaves (32 servings).

Nutrition facts per serving: 112 calories, 4 g total fat (2 g saturated fat), 9 mg cholesterol, 135 mg sodium, 15 g carbohydrate, 1 g fiber, 4 g protein.
***Daily value:** 3% vitamin A, 5% vitamin C, 6% calcium, 6% iron.*

HERBED CHEESE WHOLE WHEAT BREAD STICKS

Lots of flavor is packed into these cheesy bread sticks seasoned with oregano. Try different herbs, such as rosemary, basil, or thyme, to complement your main dish.

½ to ¾ cup all-purpose flour
1 package active dry yeast
½ cup warm water (120° to 130°)
1 tablespoon honey
1 tablespoon cooking oil
½ teaspoon salt
¾ cup whole wheat flour
1 tablespoon grated Parmesan cheese
½ teaspoon dried oregano, crushed
1 slightly beaten egg white
1 tablespoon grated Parmesan cheese
½ teaspoon dried oregano, crushed

In a large mixing bowl stir together ½ *cup* all-purpose flour and the yeast. Add water, honey, oil, and salt. Beat with an electric mixer on low speed for 30 seconds, scraping sides of bowl constantly. Beat on high speed for 3 minutes. Using a wooden spoon, stir in whole wheat flour, 1 tablespoon Parmesan cheese, ½ teaspoon oregano, and as much of the remaining all-purpose flour as you can.

Turn the dough out on a lightly floured surface. Knead in enough of the remaining all-purpose flour to make a moderately soft dough that is smooth and elastic (6 to 8 minutes total). Shape into a ball. Place in a lightly greased bowl, turning once to grease surface. Cover and let rise in a warm place till double (about 1 hour).

Punch dough down. Turn dough out onto a lightly floured surface. Cover and let rest for 10 minutes. Lightly grease two baking sheets.

Roll dough into a 15x7-inch rectangle. Cut into fifteen 1-inch strips. Place strips on prepared baking sheets. (If desired, twist each strip 3 to 4 turns, stretching gently to form 10-inch-long twisted bread sticks. Place on prepared baking sheets and press ends to baking sheet.) Cover and let rise in warm place till nearly double (about 30 minutes). Brush bread sticks with egg white. In a small mixing bowl stir together 1 tablespoon Parmesan cheese and ½ teaspoon oregano. Sprinkle over bread sticks.

Bake in a 375° oven about 12 minutes or till golden brown. Remove from baking sheets. Cool on wire racks. Makes 15 bread sticks.

Nutrition facts per serving: 53 calories, 1 g total fat (0 g saturated fat), 1 mg cholesterol, 91 mg sodium, 9 g carbohydrate, 1 g fiber, 2 g protein.
Daily value: 0% vitamin A, 0% vitamin C, 1% calcium, 3% iron.

BEST-EVER CINNAMON ROLLS

Mix, fill, and shape these gooey cinnamon rolls the night before. In the morning, bake and enjoy.

4½ to 5 cups all-purpose flour
1 package active dry yeast
1 cup milk
⅓ cup butter or margarine
⅓ cup granulated sugar
½ teaspoon salt
3 eggs
¾ cup packed brown sugar
¼ cup all-purpose flour
1 tablespoon ground cinnamon
½ cup butter or margarine
½ cup light raisins
½ cup chopped pecans or walnuts
1 tablespoon half-and-half or
   light cream
   Vanilla Icing (see recipe, page 97)

In a mixing bowl stir together *2¼ cups* of the flour and the yeast. In a saucepan heat and stir milk, ⅓ cup butter, ⅓ cup granulated sugar, and salt just till warm (120° to 130°). Add to flour mixture. Add eggs. Beat with an electric mixer on low speed for 30 seconds, scraping the sides of bowl constantly. Beat on high speed for 3 minutes. Stir in as much of the remaining flour as you can.

On a lightly floured surface, knead in enough of the remaining flour to make a moderately soft dough that is smooth and elastic (3 to 5 minutes total). Shape the dough into a ball. Place dough in a lightly greased bowl, turning once to grease surface of the dough. Cover and let rise in a warm place till double (about 1 hour). Meanwhile, for filling, combine brown sugar, the ¼ cup flour, and cinnamon. Cut in ½ cup butter till crumbly and set aside.

Punch dough down on a lightly floured surface. Cover and let rest for 10 minutes. Roll the dough into a 12-inch square. Sprinkle filling over dough, top with raisins and pecans. Roll up jelly-roll style. Slice roll into eight 1-inch pieces. Arrange dough pieces, cut side up, in a greased 12-inch deep-dish pizza pan. Cover with oiled waxed paper, then with plastic wrap, and refrigerate for 2 to 24 hours.

Let stand at room temperature about 30 minutes. Puncture any surface bubbles with a greased wooden toothpick. Brush dough with half-and-half. Bake in a 375° oven for 25 to 30 minutes or till golden brown. Remove rolls from oven. Brush again with half-and-half. Cool for 1 minute. Invert rolls on a wire rack. Cool slightly. Invert again onto a serving platter. Drizzle with Vanilla Icing. Makes 8 rolls.

Nutrition facts per roll: 690 calories, 27 g total fat (13 g saturated fat), 135 mg cholesterol, 376 mg sodium, 103 g carbohydrate, 3 g fiber, 12 g protein.
Daily value: 23% vitamin A, 1% vitamin C, 8% calcium, 30% iron.

SOFT PRETZELS

Soft and chewy, these homemade pretzels are a treat. Try dipping in yellow mustard for a hearty snack.

3   to 3¼ cups all-purpose flour
1   package active dry yeast
1   cup milk
1   tablespoon sugar
½   teaspoon salt
2   tablespoons salt
3   quarts water
1   slightly beaten egg white
1   tablespoon water
    Coarse salt, sesame seed,
       or poppy seed

In a large mixing bowl stir together *1 cup* of the flour and yeast. In a saucepan heat and stir milk, sugar, and ½ teaspoon salt just till warm (120° to 130°). Add to flour mixture. Beat with an electric mixer on low speed for 30 seconds. Beat on high speed for 3 minutes. Stir in as much of the remaining flour as you can.

Knead in enough of the remaining flour to make a moderately soft dough that is smooth and elastic (6 to 8 minutes total). Place dough in a lightly greased bowl; turn to grease surface of dough. Cover and let rise in a warm place till double (about 1¼ hours).

Punch dough down on a lightly floured surface. Cover and let rest for 10 minutes. Roll dough into a 12x10-inch rectangle. Cut into twelve 10x1-inch strips. Pull each strip about 16 inches long. Shape by crossing one end over the other to form a circle, overlapping about 4 inches from ends. Twist once where dough overlaps. Lift ends across to the opposite edge of the circle; tuck ends under edges. Press to seal. Place on greased baking sheets. Bake in a 475° oven about 4 minutes. Remove from oven. Lower oven temperature to 350°.

Dissolve the 2 tablespoons salt in 3 quarts boiling water. Lower the pretzels, three at a time, into boiling water. Boil for 2 minutes, turning once. Remove pretzels and drain on paper towels. Let stand a few seconds, then place about ½ inch apart on well-greased baking sheets. Combine egg white and the 1 tablespoon water. Brush pretzels with the egg mixture. Sprinkle pretzels lightly with coarse salt. Bake in a 350° oven for 25 to 30 minutes or till golden brown. Remove from baking sheets. Cool on wire racks. Makes 12 pretzels.

Nutrition facts per pretzel: 122 calories, 1 g total fat (0 g saturated fat), 2 mg cholesterol, 371 mg sodium, 24 g carbohydrate, 1 g fiber, 4 g protein.
Daily value: 1% vitamin A, 0% vitamin C, 2% calcium, 9% iron.

PROSCIUTTO BREAD

For two smaller loaves, prepare as directed except divide into two balls before the 10-minute rest period. Roll each ball into a 12x10-inch rectangle and reduce second baking time by 10 minutes.

½ cup chopped onion
1 tablespoon olive oil or cooking oil
½ cup sun-dried tomatoes (dry-pack or oil-pack)
3 to 3½ cups all-purpose flour
1 package active dry yeast
2 teaspoons fennel seed, crushed
¼ to ½ teaspoon pepper
¼ teaspoon salt
¾ cup warm water (120° to 130°)
2 beaten eggs
4 ounces thinly sliced prosciutto or Canadian-style bacon, finely chopped (1 cup)
Cornmeal
1 beaten egg white
1 teaspoon water

In a skillet cook the onion in oil over medium-low heat for 6 to 8 minutes or till tender. Set aside. Place dry-pack tomatoes in a bowl and pour boiling water over to cover. Let stand 2 minutes. Drain and snip tomatoes. If using oil-pack tomatoes, drain and snip. Set aside.

In a mixing bowl stir together *1¼ cups* of the flour, yeast, fennel, pepper, and salt. Add ¾ cup warm water to flour mixture. Add eggs. Beat with an electric mixer on low speed for 30 seconds, scraping the sides of the bowl. Beat on high speed for 3 minutes. Stir in onion, tomatoes, prosciutto, and as much of the remaining flour as you can.

On a lightly floured surface, knead in enough of the remaining flour to make a soft dough that is smooth and elastic (8 to 10 minutes). Place dough in a lightly greased bowl, turning once to grease surface of the dough. Cover and let rise in a warm place till double (1 hour).

Punch dough down on a lightly floured surface. Cover and let rest for 10 minutes. Lightly grease a baking sheet and sprinkle with cornmeal. Roll dough into a 15x10-inch rectangle. Roll up, jelly-roll style. Place, seam side down, on baking sheet. Cover and let rise in a warm place till nearly double (for 30 to 40 minutes).

Combine egg white and 1 teaspoon water. Brush mixture on loaf. Using a sharp knive make 6 diagonal cuts ¼ inch deep across top and repeat in opposite direction. Bake in a 375° oven about 20 minutes. Brush loaf again with egg white mixture. Bake for 15 to 20 minutes more or till bread sounds hollow when you tap the top with your fingers. Remove from baking sheet. Makes 1 loaf (20 servings).

Nutrition facts per serving: 104 calories, 3 g total fat (0 g saturated fat), 21 mg cholesterol, 165 mg sodium, 15 g carbohydrate, 1 g fiber, 4 g protein.
Daily value: *1% vitamin A, 1% vitamin C, 0% calcium, 6% iron.*

DANISH-STYLE ROLLS

Rich and buttery breakfast rolls make any occasion special. The secret to their delicate flaky texture is keeping the dough cold while you work.

3¾ cups all-purpose flour
  1 package active dry yeast
  1 cup milk
  ⅓ cup sugar
  ¼ cup water
  ½ teaspoon salt
  1 egg
  1 cup chilled butter
  ¾ cup strawberry, apricot, or pineapple
      preserves
  1 beaten egg
  1 tablespoon water
      Vanilla Icing

In a bowl combine *2 cups* flour and the yeast. In a saucepan heat milk, sugar, water, and salt till warm (120° to 130°). Add to flour mixture. Add egg. Beat on low to medium speed for 30 seconds, scraping the bowl constantly. Beat on high speed for 3 minutes. Stir in the remaining flour. Cover and refrigerate for 15 minutes.

On a floured surface (dough will be soft), knead dough gently 10 to 12 strokes. Roll into an 18x15-inch rectangle. Cut ⅓ *cup* butter into small pieces. Dot dough with butter. Fold lengthwise into thirds and then fold crosswise into thirds. Wrap and refrigerate 15 minutes. Repeat dotting with butter, folding, and chilling procedure twice more.

Divide dough in half. On a lightly floured surface, place one portion of the dough. Wrap and refrigerate remaining dough till ready to use. Roll out the dough into a 10x12-inch rectangle. Cut crosswise into ten 12x1-inch rectangles. Spoon *2 teaspoons* preserves onto the center of each rectangle. Brush edges of rectangle with a mixture of egg and 1 tablespoon water. Fold short sides of rectangles over filling to overlap in the center. Pinch edges together to seal. Place seam-side down on baking sheet. Repeat shaping with remaining portions. Cover and let rise in a warm place till nearly double (45 minutes to 1 hour).

Bake in a 375° oven for 14 to 16 minutes or till golden brown. Cool on wire racks. Drizzle with Vanilla Icing. Makes 16 rolls.

Vanilla Icing: In bowl combine ½ cup sifted *powdered sugar*, 1 tablespoon *milk*, and ½ teaspoon *vanilla*. Stir till smooth.

Nutrition facts per roll: 282 calories, 13 g total fat (8 g saturated fat), 59 mg cholesterol, 201 mg sodium, 38 g carbohydrate, 1 g fiber, 4 g protein.
Daily value: 12% vitamin A, 0% vitamin C, 2% calcium, 10% iron.

ONION MUSTARD SANDWICH BUNS

For frankfurter buns, shape dough portions into 4- to 5-inch-long rolls, tapering ends. Place on greased baking sheets and flatten each with palm of hand. Bake as for round-shaped buns.

5¼ to 5¾ cups all-purpose flour
  1 package active dry yeast
  2 cups milk
  2 tablespoons sugar
  2 tablespoons cooking oil
  2 tablespoons prepared mustard
  2 tablespoons instant minced onion
  1 teaspoon salt
  ½ teaspoon freshly ground pepper
  1 egg
  1 beaten egg
  2 tablespoons water
  4 teaspoons instant minced onion

In a bowl combine *2 cups* of flour and yeast. In a saucepan heat and stir milk, sugar, oil, mustard, 2 tablespoons instant minced onion, salt, and pepper just till warm (120° to 130°). Add milk mixture to flour mixture. Add 1 egg. Beat on low to medium speed for 30 seconds, scraping the bowl. Then beat on high for 3 minutes. Using a wooden spoon, stir in as much of the remaining flour as you can.

On a lightly floured surface knead in enough of the remaining flour to make a moderately soft dough that is smooth and elastic (6 to 8 minutes total). Shape the dough into a ball. Place dough in a lightly greased bowl, turning once to grease surface of the dough. Cover and let rise in a warm place till double (about 1 hour).

Punch dough down. Turn dough out onto a lightly floured surface. Divide dough in half. Cover and let rest for 10 minutes. Meanwhile, lightly grease two baking sheets.

Pat each portion of the dough into a 9-inch square. Cut into nine 3-inch squares. Tuck corners under to form balls. Place on the prepared baking sheets. Flatten each with palm of your hand. Cover and let rise in a warm place till nearly double (for 30 to 40 minutes).

In a bowl combine egg and 2 tablespoons water. Brush buns with some of the egg mixture. Bake in a 350°oven about 20 minutes. Brush buns again with egg mixture and sprinkle with 4 teaspoons instant minced onion. Bake 5 minutes more or till buns are golden and onion is toasted. Remove buns from baking sheets. Cool on wire racks. Makes 18.

Nutrition facts per bun: 169 calories, 3 g total fat (1 g saturated fat), 26 mg cholesterol, 162 mg sodium, 29 g carbohydrate, 1 g fiber, 5 g protein.
Daily value: 2% vitamin A, 1% vitamin C, 3% calcium, 11% iron.

CHEDDAR BATTER BREAD

Batter breads are a quick way to a homemade loaf of yeast bread. There is no kneading and they require just one rising time. Mix and let rise in baking pan.

1   tablespoon cornmeal
2   cups all-purpose flour
1   package active dry yeast
¼   teaspoon onion powder
¼   teaspoon pepper
1   cup milk
2   tablespoons sugar
2   tablespoons butter or margarine
¼   teaspoon salt
1   egg
¾   cup shredded cheddar or Monterey
     Jack cheese with jalapeño peppers
     (3 ounces)
½   cup cornmeal

Grease an 8x4x2-inch loaf pan and sprinkle with the 1 tablespoon cornmeal. Set aside.

In a large mixing bowl stir together *1½ cups* of the flour, the yeast, onion powder, and pepper. In a small saucepan heat and stir milk, sugar, butter or margarine, and salt just till warm (120° to 130°) and butter or margarine almost melts. Add milk mixture to flour mixture. Add the egg. Beat with an electric mixer on low to medium speed for 30 seconds, scraping the sides of the bowl constantly. Then beat on high speed for 3 minutes. Using a wooden spoon, stir in cheese, ½ cup cornmeal, and remaining flour. (The batter will be soft and sticky.)

Turn the batter into the prepared pan. Cover and let rise in a warm place till nearly double (about 1 hour).

Bake in a 350° oven about 40 minutes or till bread sounds hollow when you tap the top with your fingers. (If necessary, cover loosely with foil the last 15 minutes of baking to prevent overbrowning.) Immediately remove bread from pan. Cool on wire rack. Makes 1 loaf (16 servings).

Nutrition facts per serving: 124 calories, 4 g total fat (2 g saturated fat), 24 mg cholesterol, 93 mg sodium, 17 g carbohydrate, 1 g fiber, 4 g protein.
Daily value: 4% vitamin A, 0% vitamin C, 5% calcium, 6% iron.

COUNTRY RYE BREAD

The Rye Sponge method gives this bread a slightly tangy taste and a chewy, crusty surface. This rustic loaf goes well with any hearty homemade soup.

4 to 4½ cups bread flour
1 package active dry yeast
2 cups warm water (120° to 130°)
Rye Sponge (recipe follows)
2 teaspoons salt
1½ cups rye flour
1 egg white
1 tablespoon flour
½ teaspoon poppy seed

In a bowl stir together *2 cups* of bread flour and yeast. Add 2 cups warm water to flour mixture. Beat on low speed for 30 seconds. Beat on high speed for 3 minutes. Stir in Rye Sponge and salt till smooth. Stir in rye flour and as much of the remaining bread flour as you can.

Knead in enough of the remaining bread flour to make a moderately soft dough that is smooth and elastic (8 to 10 minutes total). Place dough in a greased bowl, turning once to grease surface of the dough. Cover and let rise in a warm place till double (30 to 40 minutes).

Punch dough down. Divide dough in half. Cover and let rest for 10 minutes. Lightly grease one large baking sheet. Shape dough into 2 round loaves. Place on a baking sheet. Flatten to a 6-inch diameter. Cover and let rise in a warm place till nearly double (30 minutes).

Make crisscross slashes across tops of loaves. Brush loaves with mixture of egg white and 1 tablespoon water. Sprinkle with poppy seed. Bake in a 375° oven about 40 minutes or till bread sounds hollow when you tap the top with your fingers. Remove bread from baking sheet. Cool on wire racks. Makes 2 loaves (32 to 36 servings).

Rye Sponge: In a bowl combine 1 tablespoon *honey* and 1 cup *warm water* (105° to 115°). Add 1 package *active dry yeast* and stir to dissolve. Let stand 10 minutes. Stir in 1 cup *rye flour* till mixed. Stir in enough *bread flour* (about 1 to 1½ cups) so mixture is stiff enough to knead. On a lightly floured surface, knead 3 minutes, adding more bread flour if sticky. Place in bowl. Cover with oiled waxed paper, then plastic wrap and let stand at room temperature overnight.

Nutrition facts per serving: 110 calories, 1 g total fat (0 g saturated fat), 0 mg cholesterol, 136 mg sodium, 22 g carbohydrate, 2 g fiber, 4 g protein.
Daily value: 0% vitamin A, 0% vitamin C, 0% calcium, 7% iron.

WALNUT BREAD

This recipe turns out four loaves of bread swirled with a sugared walnut filling. Delicious topped with thinly sliced ham or smoked turkey and cream cheese.

1¼ cups warm water (105° to 115°)
2 packages active dry yeast
1 teaspoon granulated sugar
6¼ to 6¾ cups all-purpose flour
⅔ cup granulated sugar
1 teaspoon salt
⅓ cup butter or margarine, melted
1 tablespoon shortening, melted
2 beaten eggs
1 12-ounce can evaporated milk (1½ cups)
4 cups ground walnuts (1 pound)
⅔ cup packed brown sugar
⅓ cup granulated sugar
½ teaspoon vanilla
3 tablespoons butter or margarine, softened
1 beaten egg
1 tablespoon milk

In a bowl combine water, yeast, and 1 teaspoon granulated sugar and stir to dissolve yeast. In another bowl stir together *2 cups* of the flour, ⅔ cup granulated sugar, and salt. Make a well in the center. Add ⅓ cup butter and shortening. Stir in 2 eggs. Stir in yeast mixture and ¾ cup evaporated milk. Beat on low speed for 30 seconds. Beat on high speed for 3 minutes. Stir in as much remaining flour as you can.

On a lightly floured surface, knead in enough remaining flour to make a moderately soft dough that is smooth and elastic (3 to 5 minutes total). Place dough in a lightly greased bowl, turning once to grease surface of the dough. Cover and let rise in a warm place till double (about 1 hour). For filling, in a mixing bowl stir together walnuts, brown sugar, ⅓ cup granulated sugar, and vanilla. Stir in 3 tablespoons softened butter and enough of the remaining evaporated milk (about ¼ cup) to make a mixture that is easy to spread.

Punch dough down on a lightly floured surface. Divide dough into 4 portions. Cover and let rest 10 minutes. Roll one portion of dough into a 16x10-inch rectangle. Dot rectangle with *⅔ cup* of the filling and spread evenly to edges. Roll up loosely, jelly-roll style, from one of the long edges. (If rolled too tightly, the filling may cause the dough to crack during baking.) Moisten edges and pinch to seal. Repeat with remaining dough and filling to make 3 more loaves. Place loaves, seam-side down, on a greased baking sheet. Prick tops with a fork. In a bowl stir together 1 egg and the milk and brush mixture on dough. Bake in a 350° oven for 30 to 35 minutes or till breads sound hollow when you tap the tops with your fingers. Cool on a wire rack. Makes 4 loaves (64 servings).

Nutrition facts per serving: 132 calories, 7 g total fat (2 g saturated fat), 16 mg cholesterol, 59 mg sodium, 16 g carbohydrate, 1 g fiber, 3 g protein.
Daily value: 2% vitamin A, 0% vitamin C, 2% calcium, 5% iron.

WHOLE WHEAT RAISIN CINNAMON ROLLS

If you don't have two 13x9x2-inch baking pans, place half of the rolls into two 9-inch round cake pans or bake individually on greased baking sheets.

1½ cups light raisins
2 cups boiling water
⅓ cup butter or margarine
3 to 3½ cups all-purpose flour
2 packages active dry yeast
½ teaspoon salt
½ cup honey
2 beaten eggs
3 cups whole wheat flour
¼ cup butter or margarine, melted
Cinnamon Pecan Filling
Butter Icing

In a bowl stir raisins and boiling water. Let stand 10 minutes. Drain, reserving liquid. (Add water to make 1⅔ cups.) Add ⅓ cup butter to liquid, cool to 120° to 130°. In bowl stir *2 cups* all-purpose flour, yeast, and salt. Add butter mixture, honey, and eggs. Beat for 30 seconds. Beat on high speed for 3 minutes. Stir in raisins, whole wheat flour, and as much of the remaining all-purpose flour as you can.

On a lightly floured surface, knead in enough of the remaining flour to make a moderately soft dough that is smooth and elastic (3 to 5 minutes total). Place dough in a lightly greased bowl; turn to grease surface of the dough. Cover and let rise in a warm place till double (about 1 hour). Punch dough down. Divide dough in half. Cover and let rest for 10 minutes. Lightly grease two 13x9x2-inch baking pans.

Roll one portion of the dough into a 15x10-inch rectangle. Brush with *2 tablespoons* butter and sprinkle with half of the Cinnamon Pecan Filling. Roll up, jelly-roll style. Cut into 12 slices. Repeat with remaining dough. Place slices in the pan. Cover and let rise in a warm place till double (30 to 40 minutes). Bake in a 375° oven about 30 minutes or till golden brown. Remove from pans. Cool on wire racks. Drizzle warm rolls with Butter Icing. Serve warm. Makes 30.

Cinnamon Pecan Filling: In bowl combine 1¼ cups packed *brown sugar*, ½ cup *toasted wheat germ*, 1 tablespoon *ground cinnamon*, and 1 cup *chopped pecans*.

Butter Icing: Mix 3 cups sifted *powdered sugar*, ¼ cup *soft butter*, and enough *milk* (4 to 6 tablespoons) to make desired consistency. Stir till smooth.

Nutrition facts per roll: 275 calories, 8 g total fat (4 g saturated fat), 28 mg cholesterol, 97 mg sodium, 48 g carbohydrate, 2 g fiber, 5 g protein.
Daily value: 5% vitamin A, 0% vitamin C, 2% calcium, 12% iron.

PARMESAN BATTER ROLLS

If you'd like to use paper bake cups, go ahead. They make pan cleanup easier and give a special touch to these brioche-type rolls.

2½   cups all-purpose flour
1   package active dry yeast
1   cup milk
½   cup butter or margarine
¼   cup sugar
½   teaspoon salt
1   egg
½   cup grated Parmesan cheese
    Sesame seed or grated Parmesan
      cheese

In a large mixing bowl stir together *2 cups* of the flour and the yeast. In a medium saucepan heat and stir milk, butter or margarine, sugar, and salt just till warm (120° to 130°) and butter almost melts. Add milk mixture to flour mixture. Add egg and ½ cup Parmesan cheese. Beat with an electric mixer on low to medium speed for 30 seconds, scraping the sides of the bowl constantly. Then beat on high speed for 3 minutes. Using a wooden spoon, stir in remaining flour. Cover and let rise in a warm place till double (about 1 hour).

Grease sixteen 2½-inch muffin pan cups. Spoon batter into muffin pan cups, filling ⅔ full. Cover and let rise in a warm place till nearly double (about 30 minutes). Sprinkle with sesame seed or additional Parmesan cheese.

Bake in a 350° oven for 20 to 25 minutes or till golden brown. Immediately remove rolls from pan and serve warm. Makes 16.

Nutrition facts per roll: 158 calories, 8 g total fat (4 g saturated fat), 32 mg cholesterol, 195 mg sodium, 18 g carbohydrate, 1 g fiber, 4 g protein.
Daily value: 7% vitamin A, 0% vitamin C, 5% calcium, 6% iron.

WHOLE WHEAT PITA

Steam makes a hollow in the center of these Middle Eastern breads—perfect for stuffing with thinly sliced meats, cheeses, and vegetables.

1¼ to 1¾ cups all-purpose flour
1 package active dry yeast
1¼ cups water
2 tablespoons shortening, butter,
    or margarine
¾ teaspoon salt
2 cups whole wheat flour

In a bowl stir together *1¼ cups* of the all-purpose flour and yeast. In a saucepan heat and stir water, shortening, and salt till just warm (120° to 130°). Add to flour mixture. Beat on low speed for 30 seconds. Beat on high speed for 3 minutes. Stir in whole wheat flour and as much of the remaining all-purpose flour as you can.

On a lightly floured surface, knead in enough of the remaining all-purpose flour to make a moderately soft dough that is smooth and elastic (3 to 5 minutes total). Cover and let rest in a warm place for 15 minutes. Divide dough into 12 portions. Roll each dough portion into a very smooth ball. Cover dough balls with a damp cloth and let rest for 10 minutes. Flatten balls with your fingers. Cover and let rest for 10 minutes. (Keep the dough balls covered till ready to use.)

Roll one dough ball into a 7-inch round, turn dough over once while rolling. Roll dough from center to edge. Do not stretch, puncture, or crease dough. Repeat rolling with another ball of dough. (Work with enough flour on the surface so that the dough does not stick.)

Place two dough rounds on a preheated ungreased baking sheet. Bake in a 450° oven about 3 minutes or till bread is puffed and softly set. Turn over with a wide spatula. Bake about 2 minutes more or till bread begins to lightly brown. Cool slightly on a wire rack. While still warm, place bread in a paper sack or plastic bag to keep it soft and prevent it from drying out. Repeat with remaining dough, baking one batch before rolling and baking the next batch. To serve, cut each pita crosswise. Open halves and fill as desired. Makes 12.

Nutrition facts per pita: 130 calories, 2 g total fat (1 g saturated fat), 5 mg cholesterol, 155 mg sodium, 24 g carbohydrate, 3 g fiber, 4 g protein.
Daily value: 1% vitamin A, 0% vitamin C, 0% calcium, 9% iron.

WHEAT SWIRL BREAD

This recipe turns out six miniature-size loaves, perfect for open-face sandwiches for appetizers or teatime.

4½ to 5 cups all-purpose flour
2 packages active dry yeast
2 cups milk
½ cup honey
¼ cup butter or margarine
1 teaspoon salt
1 egg
1 cup whole wheat flour
½ cup rye flour
½ cup toasted wheat germ
¼ cup butter or margarine, softened
⅔ cup packed brown sugar

In a mixing bowl stir together *2 cups* of the all-purpose flour and the yeast. In a saucepan heat and stir milk, honey, ¼ cup butter, and salt just till warm (120° to 130°). Add milk mixture to flour mixture. Add egg. Beat with an electric mixer on low to medium speed for 30 seconds, scraping the sides of the bowl constantly. Beat on high speed for 3 minutes. Stir in whole wheat flour, rye flour, wheat germ, and as much of the remaining all-purpose flour as you can.

On a lightly floured surface, knead in enough of the remaining all-purpose flour to make a moderately soft dough that is smooth and elastic (6 to 8 minutes total). Shape the dough into a ball. Place dough in a lightly greased bowl, turning once to grease the surface. Cover and let rise in a warm place till double (about 1¼ hours).

Punch dough down on a lightly floured surface. Divide dough in half. Cover and let rest for 10 minutes. Lightly grease six 5½x3x2-inch loaf pans.

Roll one portion of the dough into a 15-inch square. Spread with 2 tablespoons of the softened butter and sprinkle with ⅓ cup of the brown sugar. Tightly roll up, jelly-roll style. Seal with fingertips as you roll. Cut into thirds. Repeat with remaining dough. Place the shaped dough in the prepared loaf pans. Cover and let rise in a warm place till nearly double (about 45 minutes).

Bake in a 350° oven about 30 minutes or till bread sounds hollow when you tap the top with your fingers. Immediately remove bread from pans. Cool on wire racks. Makes 6 loaves (48 servings).

Nutrition facts per serving: 100 calories, 2 g total fat (1 g saturated fat), 10 mg cholesterol, 71 mg sodium, 17 g carbohydrate, 1 g fiber, 3 g protein.
Daily value: 2% vitamin A, 0% vitamin C, 1% calcium, 5% iron.

CLOVERLEAF RYE ROLLS

To make these rolls ahead, wrap the cooled, baked rolls in a single layer of heavy foil. Seal, label, and freeze up to 2 months. To reheat, place baked wrapped rolls in a 350° oven 30 to 35 minutes.

3½ to 4 cups all-purpose flour
  2 packages active dry yeast
 ¼ cup sugar
  1 teaspoon salt
  2 cups water
  2 tablespoons shortening
  2 cups rye flour
    Melted butter or margarine (optional)

In a large mixing bowl stir together *2¾ cups* of the all-purpose flour, the yeast, sugar, and salt. In a medium saucepan heat and stir water and shortening just till warm (120° to 130°) and shortening almost melts. Add shortening mixture to flour mixture. Beat with an electric mixer on low to medium speed for 30 seconds, scraping the sides of the bowl constantly. Then beat on high speed for 3 minutes. Using a wooden spoon, stir in rye flour and as much of the remaining all-purpose flour as you can.

Turn the dough out onto a lightly floured surface. Knead in enough of the remaining all-purpose flour to make a moderately soft dough that is smooth and elastic (6 to 8 minutes total). Shape the dough into a ball. Place dough in a lightly greased bowl, turning once to grease surface of the dough. Cover and let rise in a warm place till double (about 1 hour).

Punch dough down. Turn dough out onto lightly floured surface. Divide dough in half. Cover and let rest for 10 minutes. Meanwhile, lightly grease twenty-four 2½-inch muffin cups.

Divide each portion of the dough into 36 pieces. Shape each piece into a ball, pulling edges under to make a smooth top. Place 3 balls in each muffin cup, smooth side up. Cover and let rise in a warm place till nearly double (about 30 minutes).

Bake in a 375° oven 15 to 18 minutes or till golden. If desired, brush with melted butter or margarine. Remove from pans. Cool on wire racks or serve warm. Makes 24 rolls.

Nutrition facts per roll: 110 calories, 1 g total fat (0 g saturated fat), 0 mg cholesterol, 90 mg sodium, 22 g carbohydrate, 2 g fiber, 3 g protein.
Daily value: 0% vitamin A, 0% vitamin C, 0% calcium, 7% iron.

HONEY ANISE BREAD

Aniseed gives this crusty, family-pleasing bread a light licorice flavor.

5¼ to 5¾ cups all-purpose flour
2 packages active dry yeast
½ cup honey
3 tablespoons butter or margarine
1 teaspoon salt
2¼ cups water
1 cup whole wheat flour
½ cup cracked wheat
3 tablespoons aniseed, crushed

In a bowl stir together *2 cups* of the all-purpose flour and the yeast. In a saucepan heat and stir honey, butter, salt, and water just till warm (120° to 130°). Add honey mixture to flour mixture. Beat on low speed for 30 seconds. Beat on high speed for 3 minutes. Stir in whole wheat flour, cracked wheat, aniseed, and as much of the remaining all-purpose flour as you can.

On a lightly floured surface, knead in enough of the remaining all-purpose flour to make a moderately soft dough that is smooth and elastic (6 to 8 minutes total). Shape the dough into a ball. Place dough in a lightly greased bowl, turning once to grease surface of the dough. Cover and let rise in a warm place till double (about 45 minutes). Punch dough down. Divide dough in half. Cover and let rest for 10 minutes. Meanwhile, lightly grease two 8x4x2-inch loaf pans.

Shape each portion of the dough into a loaf by patting or rolling. To shape dough by patting, gently pull dough into a loaf shape, tucking edges beneath. To shape dough by rolling, on a lightly floured surface, roll each half into a 12x8-inch rectangle. Tightly roll up, jelly-roll style, starting from one of the short sides. Seal with fingertips as you roll. Place the shaped dough in the prepared loaf pans. Cover and let rise in a warm place till double (for 30 to 40 minutes).

Bake in a 375° oven about 40 minutes or till bread sounds hollow when you tap the top with your fingers. (If necessary, cover loosely with foil the last 10 minutes of baking to prevent overbrowning.) Immediately remove bread from pans. Cool on wire racks. Makes 2 loaves (32 servings).

Nutrition facts per serving: 115 calories, 1 g total fat (1 g saturated fat), 3 mg cholesterol, 79 mg sodium, 23 g carbohydrate, 1 g fiber, 3 g protein.
Daily value: *0% vitamin A, 0% vitamin C, 0% calcium, 9% iron.*

ALASKAN SOURDOUGH BISCUITS

Taste these tender yet hearty biscuits and you'll know why the gold prospectors took sourdough starter on their trek to Alaska.

 1   cup Alaskan Sourdough Starter
2¼   cups all-purpose flour
 1   tablespoon baking powder
 1   teaspoon salt
 ½   cup shortening
 ¼   cup milk

Bring Alaskan Sourdough Starter to room temperature. In a mixing bowl stir together flour, baking powder, and salt. Using a pastry blender, cut in shortening till mixture resembles coarse crumbs. Make a well in center of dry mixture, then add Alaskan Sourdough Starter and milk all at once. Stir just till moistened.

On a lightly floured surface knead dough by folding and pressing dough for 10 to 12 strokes. Pat or lightly roll dough to ½-inch thickness. Cut dough with a floured 3-inch biscuit cutter, dipping cutter into flour between cuts. Place biscuits 1 inch apart on an ungreased baking sheet. Bake in a 450° oven for 12 minutes or till golden. Remove biscuits from baking sheet and serve warm. Makes 10 to 12.

Alaskan Sourdough Starter: In a bowl dissolve 2 packages *active dry yeast* in ½ cup *warm water* (105° to 115°). Stir in 4 cups *all-purpose flour*, 3 cups *warm water* (105° to 115°), and 1 tablespoon *sugar*. Beat till smooth. Cover with cheesecloth. Let stand in a warm place overnight. The starter is ready to use in any of the sourdough recipes. (It will look bubbly and a clear liquid may rise to the top.) Stir before measuring. Pour remaining starter into a 2-quart or larger covered plastic container. Cover and refrigerate. Makes about 5 cups. To use refrigerated starter, bring desired amount to room temperature. For every 1 cup used, replenish starter by stirring in ¾ cup *all-purpose flour*, ¾ cup *warm water* (105° to 115°), and 1 teaspoon *sugar*. Cover with cheesecloth and let stand at room temperature 8 hours or overnight. Cover and refrigerate for later use. If starter isn't used within 10 days, stir in 1 teaspoon *sugar*. Repeat every 10 days unless replenished as above.

Nutrition facts per biscuit: 224 calories, 11 g total fat (3 g saturated fat), 0 mg cholesterol, 326 mg sodium, 28 g carbohydrate, 1 g fiber, 4 g protein.
Daily value: 0% vitamin A, 0% vitamin C, 9% calcium, 12% iron.

SOURDOUGH BREAD

This hearty textured bread tastes delightful when cut into thick slices and smeared with soft butter. The starter gives it a nice tangy flavor.

1 cup Alaskan Sourdough Starter
    (see recipe, page 136)
4½ to 5 cups all-purpose flour
1 package active dry yeast
1 cup milk
3 tablespoons cooking oil
1 tablespoon sugar
1 teaspoon salt
½ teaspoon baking soda
1 slightly beaten egg white
1 tablespoon water

Bring Alaskan Sourdough Starter to room temperature. In a bowl stir together *1½ cups* of the flour and the yeast. In a saucepan heat and stir milk, oil, sugar, and salt just till warm (120° to 130°). Add to flour mixture along with Alaskan Sourdough Starter. Beat on low speed for 30 seconds. Beat on high speed for 3 minutes. Combine *2 cups* flour and soda. Add to yeast mixture. Stir till combined. Stir in as much of the remaining flour as you can.

Knead in enough of the remaining flour to make a moderately soft dough that is smooth and elastic (6 to 8 minutes total). Place dough in a lightly greased bowl, turning once to grease surface of the dough. Cover and let rise in a warm place till double (45 to 60 minutes).

Punch dough down. Turn dough out onto a lightly floured surface. Divide dough in half. Cover and let rest for 10 minutes. Meanwhile, lightly grease two baking sheets. Shape each portion of the dough into two round loaves. Flatten each loaf to 7-inch diameter. Cover and let rise in a warm place till nearly double (25 to 30 minutes) Using a sharp knife, make several cuts crosswise to each other across tops of loaves. Brush loaves with a mixture of egg white and water. Place the shaped dough in the prepared loaf pans. Cover and let rise in a warm place till nearly double (25 to 30 minutes).

Bake in a 375° oven for 25 to 30 minutes or till bread sounds hollow when you tap the top with your fingers. (If necessary, cover loosely with foil the last 10 minutes of baking to prevent overbrowning.) Immediately remove bread from pans. Cool on wire racks. Makes 2 loaves (24 to 36 servings).

Nutrition facts per serving: 116 calories, 2 g total fat (0 g saturated fat), 1 mg cholesterol, 121 mg sodium, 21 g carbohydrate, 1 g fiber, 3 g protein.
Daily value: 0% vitamin A, 0% vitamin C, 1% calcium, 8% iron.

GOLD RUSH PANCAKES

You'll find a pleasant sourdough flavor in these hearty pancakes. They taste good plain or served traditionally with syrup and butter.

1   **cup Alaskan Sourdough Starter (see recipe, page 136)**
1   **cup all-purpose flour**
2   **tablespoons sugar**
1   **teaspoon baking powder**
½   **teaspoon salt**
1   **beaten egg**
½   **cup warm milk (110° to 115°)**
2   **tablespoons cooking oil**

Bring Alaskan Sourdough Starter to room temperature. In a large mixing bowl stir together flour, sugar, baking powder, and salt. In another mixing bowl combine egg, milk, oil, and Alaskan Sourdough Starter. Add to flour mixture all at once. Stir mixture just till blended but still slightly lumpy.

Pour about ¼ *cup* batter onto a hot, lightly greased griddle or heavy skillet for each standard size pancake or about *1 tablespoon* batter for each dollar-size pancake.

Cook till pancakes are golden brown, turning to cook second sides when pancakes have bubbly surfaces and slightly dry edges. Makes 8 to 10 standard-size or 36 dollar-size pancakes.

Nutrition facts per pancake: 156 calories, 5 g total fat (1 g saturated fat), 28 mg cholesterol, 195 mg sodium, 24 g carbohydrate, 1 g fiber, 4 g protein.
Daily value: 2% vitamin A, 0% vitamin C, 5% calcium, 9% iron.

Keep track of your daily nutrition needs by using the information we provide at the end of each recipe. We've analyzed the nutritional content of each recipe serving for you. When a recipe gives an ingredient substitution, we used the first choice in the analysis. If it makes a range of servings (such as 4 to 6), we used the smallest number. Ingredients listed as optional weren't included in the calculations.

METRIC COOKING HINTS

By making a few conversions, cooks in Australia, Canada, and the United Kingdom can use the recipes in Better Homes and Gardens® *Muffins & Breads* with confidence. The charts on this page provide a guide for converting measurements from the U.S. customary system, which is used throughout this book, to the imperial and metric systems. There also is a conversion table for oven temperatures to accommodate the differences in oven calibrations.

Volume and Weight: Americans traditionally use cup measures for liquid and solid ingredients. The chart (top right) shows the approximate imperial and metric equivalents. If you are accustomed to weighing solid ingredients, here are some helpful approximate equivalents:
- 1 cup butter, caster sugar, or rice = 8 ounces = about 250 grams
- 1 cup flour = 4 ounces = about 125 grams
- 1 cup icing sugar = 5 ounces = about 150 grams
  Spoon measures are used for smaller amounts of ingredients. Although the size of the tablespoon varies slightly among countries, for practical purposes and for recipes in this book, a straight substitution is all that's necessary.

  Measurements made using cups or spoons should always be level, unless stated otherwise.

Product Differences: Most of the ingredients called for in the recipes in this book are available in English-speaking countries. However, some are known by different names. Here are some common American ingredients and their possible counterparts:
- Sugar is granulated or caster sugar.
- Powdered sugar is icing sugar.
- All-purpose flour is plain household flour or white flour. When self-rising flour is used in place of all-purpose flour in a recipe that calls for leavening, omit the leavening agent (baking soda or baking powder) and salt.
- Light corn syrup is golden syrup.
- Cornstarch is cornflour.
- Baking soda is bicarbonate of soda.
- Vanilla is vanilla essence.
- Green, red, or yellow sweet peppers are capsicums.
- Sultanas are golden raisins.

USEFUL EQUIVALENTS: U.S = AUST./BR.

⅛ teaspoon = 0.5 ml
¼ teaspoon = 1 ml
½ teaspoon = 2 ml
1 teaspoon = 5 ml
1 tablespoon = 1 tablespoon
¼ cup = 2 tablespoons = 2 fluid ounces = 60 ml
⅓ cup = ¼ cup = 3 fluid ounces = 90 ml
½ cup = ⅓ cup = 4 fluid ounces = 120 ml

⅔ cup = ½ cup = 5 fluid ounces = 150 ml
¾ cup = ⅔ cup = 6 fluid ounces = 180 ml
1 cup = ¾ cup = 8 fluid ounces = 240 ml
1¼ cups = 1 cup
2 cups = 1 pint
1 quart = 1 litre
½ inch = 1.27 centimetres
1 inch = 2.54 centimetres

BAKING PAN SIZES

American	Metric
8x1½-inch round baking pan	20x4-centimetre cake tin
9x1½-inch round baking pan	23x3.5-centimetre cake tin
11x7x1½-inch baking pan	28x18x4-centimetre baking tin
13x9x2-inch baking pan	30x20x3-centimetre baking tin
2-quart rectangular baking dish	30x20x3-centimetre baking tin
15x10x2-inch baking pan	30x25x2-centimetre baking tin (Swiss roll tin)
9-inch pie plate	22x4- or 23x4-centimetre pie plate
7- or 8-inch springform pan	18- or 20-centimetre springform or loose-bottom cake tin
9x5x3-inch loaf pan	23x13x7-centimetre or 2-pound narrow loaf tin or paté tin
1½-quart casserole	1.5-litre casserole
2-quart casserole	2-litre casserole

OVEN TEMPERATURE EQUIVALENTS

Fahrenheit Setting	Celsius Setting*	Gas Setting
300°F	150°C	Gas Mark 2 (slow)
325°F	160°C	Gas Mark 3 (moderately slow)
350°F	180°C	Gas Mark 4 (moderate)
375°F	190°C	Gas Mark 5 (moderately hot)
400°F	200°C	Gas Mark 6 (hot)
425°F	220°C	Gas Mark 7
450°F	230°C	Gas Mark 8 (very hot)
Broil		Grill

Electric and gas ovens may be calibrated using Celsius. However, increase the Celsius setting 10 to 20 degrees when cooking above 160°C with an electric oven. For convection or forced-air ovens (gas or electric), lower the temperature setting 10°C when cooking at all heat levels.